Makers of History.

SIR RICHARD WHITTINGTON

LORD MAYOR OF LONDON

BY

WALTER BESANT AND JAMES RICE

"Seest thou a man diligent in his business? He shall stand before kings."

NEW YORK

MERRILL AND BAKER

PUBLISHERS

LONDON BRIDGE.

PREFACE.

THE "Life of Whittington" was originally undertaken for this series by my friend and collabora-
teur—in other lines—Mr. James Rice. With this
intention he collected a quantity of notes and materials.
Unfortunately, a long and severe illness obliged him
to throw up all but the most absolutely necessary
work. He therefore gave me over his notes, which
I have incorporated in the pages which follow; and I
have, in justice to his share in the labour, placed his
name on the title-page with my own.

As regards the materials for writing the life of
Whittington, it is necessary to acknowledge that,
although they are abundant—there is no period
which can be better understood and even restored
than the fourteenth century—it would be impossible

to produce a biography of this great merchant but for
the researches and discoveries made by the late Rev.
Samuel Lysons. They are embodied in his little
pamphlet called "The Model Merchant of the Fourteenth Century." It was he who rescued Whittington
from the realm of legend, gave him a respectable
genealogy, a birth-place, a coat of arms, brothers and
cousins, and a family history. It was Dr. Lysons
who first clearly established the antiquity of the Cat
story, and who first set forth the various claims upon
the gratitude of London established by the real facts
of this great man's life. I have ventured to differ
even from so great an antiquary in many points, and
I think he drew from his own facts, in some important
particulars, erroneous conclusions. But no one who
studies the subject can avoid consulting Lysons.
Especially I recommend the reader to study that
very curious volume which he has bequeathed to the
Guildhall Library, in which he bound up all the correspondence which followed the publication of his
book in 1859, and all the additional facts which came
to light after that publication. Not the least curious
feature in the book is the collection of letters from

persons claiming to be descendants of Whittington's brother.

After Lysons, one may consult Brewer's "Life of Carpenter;" Stow's "Survey of London;" Agas's "Map of London;" Riley's "Translation of the *Liber Albus;*" Riley's "Memorials of London;" Herbert's "History of the City Companies;" as many of the archæological works relating to old London as can be got at; the more familiar the student of the period is with Chaucer, Froissart, and Lydgate the better; and, finally, though there is little in the city to remind him of Whittington's time, he must visit the spots whose names are still the same as they were five hundred years ago, though not a stone remains to mark the site of the buildings which Whittington lived among. His church is there, re-built; the "Tower Royal" is a narrow lane; College Street marks the spot where his college stood; Mercers' Hall has still its entrance in Chepe, where was once the shop of Gilbert a Becket; Dowgate, Walbrook, Queenhithe yet survive; and in a corner below Blackfriars may still be read the name of Baynard's Castle.

I have only further to express my thanks to Mr. Watney, of the Mercers' Company, for his kindness in giving me permission to see the things which remain associated with the name of Whittington in the Mercers' Hall.

W. B

UNITED UNIVERSITIES CLUB,
July, 1881.

CONTENTS.

LIST OF ILLUSTRATIONS.

INTRODUCTION.

THE CHARTERS OF LONDON.

RICHARD WHITTINGTON, of whom we are presently to speak, was fortunate in beginning his career when London had passed through a difficult and stormy period, part of which he himself witnessed as an apprentice. What he found, when he began his course, was a city governed by officers of its own appointment, holding its own courts, brooking no interference from the King's justices, passing its own laws for the regulation and preservation of its trade, and, practically, more independent than it was to be later on, under the Tudors and Charles Stuart. The City held its freedom by right of its charters, a long series of privileges extorted from or conceded by successive kings. The most dangerous and the most imperative duty of Mayor, Sheriffs, and Aldermen was the firm maintenance of those privileges against the encroachments of Crown and Court, and the careful and ceaseless watch for such opportunity of further extension as the necessities of the King might allow. When the Sovereign was weak, so that the support of the City was needed—when his title was doubtful, so that he needed the alliance of a great town which could, on occasion, furnish an army as great as half the Barons of England could gather together—it was comparatively easy to obtain new charters and more extended privileges. When the Sovereign was firmly seated on the throne, the citizens of London, which then became an inexhaustible treasury, had to look fast to their own. The history of London may be written from many points of view. Let us here briefly consider the various charters which made London such as the city—which we have yet to describe—was when young Richard Whittington first took up his freedom, and entered upon business as a mercer and an adventurer.

On the submission of London to William the Conqueror—an event of equal importance with the battle of Senlac—he granted the burgesses a charter, the shortest perhaps ever drawn up or conceded to a city. It declared simply that every burgess of the city was law-worthy, and that every child should be his father's heir. This declaration meant a great deal more than would seem at first apparent. It acknowledged, in fact, the freedom of the City; it conceded to the people that no *seigneur* or lord could have any authority or feudal rights over them. Londoners were declared not to be "villains" living *in dominio*— on the demesne of their masters; they did not hold their lands at the risk of any feudal lord; they were not required to do service to any Baron—like, for instance, the citizens of Leicester, who, two centuries later, had to reap the corn of their Earl, to grind at his mills, to redeem their strayed cattle from his pound: their lands were their own; the fields outside their walls were their own; they could—a thing forbidden to villains—bequeath their property to their heirs, and inherit property from their fathers. This charter, in granting which William evidently recognised the importance of conciliating the wealthy and powerful City, is the document with which the modern history of London may be fairly said to begin, because it connects the government of the City with that of its former kings.

After the grant of this charter, the annals of the City show little more for some years than a record of those checks to prosperity which form the principal history of a peaceful and commercial city. In the year 1076 there is a dreadful fire ; ten years later there is another, in which St. Paul's Cathedral is destroyed. In 1090 a hurricane blew down no fewer than 600 houses in the City, with many churches, and immediately afterwards London Bridge was carried away. These things were easily repaired. A more important event for the good and evil of the City was the building of the Tower, commenced in the year 1079, and intended from the first to overawe and command the City, as well as to protect the river and the ships.

On the accession of Henry the First, the City obtained its most important charter. In this document recognition is made of the ancient privileges and customs of the citizens ; their rights are enumerated and acknowledged : they shall not be called upon to plead without the walls of the City of London ; they are to be free, scot and lot—that is, from all tolls, duties, and customs imposed upon any other part of the kingdom ; they are no longer to pay the tax of Danegelt, which still survived, though the fear of Danish invasion was fast dying out ; they are to be excused from the ordeal of battle—a privilege which shows how early common sense recognised the uncertainty of such a method of trial ; they are allowed to hunt in Middlesex and Surrey ; they are to have the right of summary execution against the goods of debtors without the walls—a very important concession to a trading community ; and they are not to have soldiers quartered upon them. The liberties granted in this charter mark the possession of a very great amount of self-government. But the granting

of a charter and the loyal adherence to its privileges
are two different things.

In the troublous reign of King Stephen, the citizens
of London, like the rest of England, suffered from the
necessity of taking a side, and the consequences of
taking the wrong side. It was the City of London
which elected Stephen at their folkmote: they swore
to defend him with money and arms; he swore to
govern well and lawfully. Seven years later, their
King, who had certainly not shown a right understanding as to the art of governing well, was defeated
and taken prisoner. Matilda rode into London in
state, and deprived the City of its liberties, granting
the sheriffwicks of Middlesex and London at a fee-
farm rent of £300 a-year, including the Tower of
London, to the Earl of Essex, and appointing him
Justiciary of the City, so that no one could hold pleas
without his consent. The City submitted; but on
Stephen's release again joined his fortunes.

Henry the Second does not seem to have entertained
animosity to the Londoners on account of their loyalty
to his rival. The City obtained a charter of privileges,
and gave large gifts to the new King, either in lieu of
tallages, or else in order to drown the memory of
their former adherence to Stephen. The withdrawal
by Matilda of rights so well defined, and already
so ancient, as those of London, could only be a
temporary measure. No king would wantonly destroy
the prosperity of this source of wealth; while the
goodwill of the City could only be obtained at the
price of the enjoyment of all its rights.

It was Henry the Second, as we shall presently
see, who claimed the right of granting permission for
Companies to establish themselves; and while he
granted charters to some trade associations, he
fined others—such as the Associated Goldsmiths,

the Pelterers, the Butchers, and others—in various considerable sums, for illegally constituting themselves into Companies. The act seems dictated by an honest desire to promote the interests of the City, because in order to render any association of workmen able to carry out its objects, it was first necessary that all of the trade should belong to it, and that it should receive legal authority to control the trade. Nothing but a royal charter could give this power. The rise of the Companies, however, and their gradual control over the whole trade of London, requires a larger consideration than these limits will allow. The discontent of the crafts and the revolutionary movement of William Fitz-Osbert belong also to this subject, and are part of the history of London in the 12th and 13th centuries. By the time of Whittington, the old causes of corruption had been removed in the final abolition of the former " magnates " or " barons " of the merchant-guild, and the substitution of a purely popular form of government through the Livery Companies. What the eloquence of William Fitz-Osbert, backed by his following of 50,000 craftsmen, failed to effect, was wrought by the silent and irresistible forces of growth and development. He fell a martyr to the cause of free government, yet the craftsmen learned from him a lesson in the art of popular movement. Nor were they ungrateful : they cut up the gibbet on which he had been hanged, and kept pieces as precious relics, powerful in healing the sick. His name of Longbeard lingered long afterwards in the minds of the lower sort, though the Church had excommunicated him, and proclaimed abroad his " numerous villainies."

The next great addition made to the liberties of the City was that granted by the charter of Richard the First, which enacted that the Keeper of the Tower of London should not have the right to exact or receive any toll on goods brought up the river, nor should "molest any person by reason of the said wares." Also, by this charter the City obtained the conservancy of the river.

In the year 1198, by the King's orders, the two Sheriffs of London provided standards of weight and measure, and sent them to all the counties.

On his accession, King John granted three charters to the citizens of London—by the first, they were exempted from paying toll in the King's foreign dominions ; by the second, they obtained power over the river Medway as well as the Thames ; by the third, they had the sheriffwicks of London and Middlesex confirmed to them at the former rent of £300 a-year, with power of choosing their own sheriffs. In another charter, dated 1202, in which, for some unexplained offence, the Weavers were expelled the City, the chief officer of the City is, for the first time, called the Mayor. The office of Chamberlain still remained in the hands of the Crown. It was bought of John, in the year 1204, by William de St. Michael, for the sum of £100 and an annual rent of 100 marks.

In the year 1209, the sheriffs, having interfered to prevent King John's purveyors carrying off a quantity of corn, were degraded and sent to the King at Langley ; but, on their representing that what they had done was to prevent an insurrection, they were pardoned and reinstated.

The Londoners were not forgotten in the Great Charter. "Let the City of London," it said, "have all its old liberties and its free customs, as well by land as by water. Besides this, we will and grant that all other cities, and boroughs, and towns, and ports have all their liberties and free customs."

The enforcement of the Charter was more difficult to procure than its signature. The barons were defeated, and withdrew into London, where the sturdy burghers disregarded Papal interdict and excommunication, had their masses and services as usual, and defied the King, until the arrival of Louis with his French troops caused the defection of John's French mercenaries. At the death of John, the Earl Mareschal confirmed the liberties of London.

But the reign of Henry III. was full of trouble to the City. During the years of misrule which followed the death of Stephen Langton, the City had to pay fines for fresh charters, fines for permission to sell a certain kind of cloth, "gifts" to the King, and even a whole fifteenth of their property. To pay a fifteenth—that is, more than $6\frac{1}{2}$ per cent. on the whole of one's possessions—appears to us almost an incredible tax. Let us imagine what such a demand would mean to an ordinary English householder of the present day. He has first to pay a fifteenth on the value of his house furniture; this, at the moderate valuation of £750, would call for a payment of £50. His books and pictures may be worth as much again; another £50 must go for them. His wife's jewels, his plate and valuables, may be set down at £300; another sum of £20 must be paid on them. Then he must pay a fifteenth on all his savings and investments, on his insurances, and, if he be a merchant or a tradesman, on his actual stock-in-trade. All this would be meant by a fifteenth; yet the citizens cheerfully accepted the tax as a part of the general burden of life's work. Better to pay a fifteenth than to have the King's justices interfering with the City and its trade.

Unfortunately, the buying of privileges never came to an end. It had to be renewed with every successive

B

king, and in the case of bad kings, as Henry III. and
Richard II., it was renewed frequently in the same
reign, the slightest disorder being seized upon as a
sufficient reason for interference. Thus, there was a
quarrel at Westminster between some of the young
citizens and some of the King's people, the cause being
a dispute about certain shootings. It was in the early
years of Henry III. A certain Constantine Fitz-
Arnulph present, a turbulent fellow, one of those who
had invited the French Prince over in the late troubles,
raised the cry of "Mountjoye St. Denis! God help
us and our Lord Louis!" For this he was hanged, he
and his son, contrary to the chartered right of every
citizen not to plead without the city. And, worse
than this, Chief-Justice Hubert went on to violate the
city liberties by entering with a strong guard, depos-
ing the Mayor, cutting off the feet of rioters, and
setting a *custos* over the city. By payment of a
heavy fine, the people got back their freedom.

Again, in the year 1224, another charter was
granted them. This was an occasion of great joy,
and it proved of so much use, that the next year
they had again to pay a fifteenth of all their goods for
the clause in their favour which had been inserted
in the confirmation of Magna Charta. Henry III.
proved a most costly king. He imposed a fifteenth
for another charter, after taking 5,000 marks from
the City; London was his treasury, from which he
thought he could draw at will, provided only that
enough was left to carry on the gold-producing
machine. Thus, on one occasion, the citizens found
that they must pay the then enormous sum of
£20,000, in order to "recover the King's favour,"
a thing which, when recovered, seemed of no advantage. Yet, when he married Eleanor, the City gave
him a splendid reception, meeting him with a troop

in which every man was dressed in silk and gold embroidery, and bore in his hand a gold or silver cup.

Henry's opinion of the City was shown when, in the year 1248, his Council at Westminster refused to grant him money, and advised him to sell his plate— the City would buy it. " If the treasure of Augustus," cried the King, " were to be sold, these Londoners would buy it." A grievous and intolerable thing, indeed, that common burgesses should grow rich in trade, while their King grew daily poorer, and was denied even the power of robbing his subjects. Yet he vexed the City continually, on one occasion creating a fair at Westminster, during which trade of every kind was to cease in London. In other words, the King enacted that no man should earn his livelihood for a fortnight. Was ever such a king known ?— save, perhaps, Caligula, or Commodus, or the mad Hakeem.

Considering the great wealth of London, its strong position, its walls and river, its large population, and the sturdy spirit of its people, it seems strange that they submitted so long. As yet, however, they knew not their strength ; they were not able to stand alone; there had been a succession of strong kings ; the time of the people had not yet come ; the internal affairs of the City were not free from discontent ; the poorer sort could not be relied upon. Therefore the Londoners were wise in their generation, and made haste to purchase, at as reasonable a rate as possible, permission to trade at fair time. Yet these traders knew already what a power might be wielded by united London ; their wars on the side of Stephen first, and the Barons afterwards, taught them their strength—a lesson which they were to learn again on the deposition of King Richard the Second.

Henry showed willingness to be conciliated. He went to live in the City at Christmas, accepted banquets, demanded New Year's gifts, exacted an additional £2,000, and encouraged his servants to take what they pleased, without payment, from the stalls. The affection of the citizens naturally grew more and more towards a king so condescending.

But worse was to follow. The charters of London seemed worth no more than the parchment on which they were written; the very means of living, to say nothing of the citizens' wealth, were at the mercy of the rapacious Sovereign; the terrified burgesses asked each other in terror what new exaction would be made. Yet they forgot one thing; no king, however mad or rapacious, would actually kill the bird which laid the golden eggs. It was necessary that London should go on accumulating wealth. The statecraft of the King's advisers was shown in rightly judging the line at which the City would allow or would resent demands for money; and year by year, in spite of these, the town grew stronger, richer, more self-reliant, yet more necessary to the Crown.

These considerations probably induced Henry to fall upon the Lombard merchants, whom he prosecuted for usury. In this way a slender supply was realised, and he then turned his attention again to the City, and proposed, with an appearance of seriousness, that the London merchants should join him in a new Crusade. The citizens allowed him to perceive that they felt scant enthusiasm about the Recovery of the Sacred Sites, whereupon the King fined them; but the Crusade was not undertaken. He seems at this time to have been deliberately bent upon humbling the City to the utmost; he multiplied frivolous, impossible, and vexatious ordinances: thus, he once ordered all the shops to be shut, and the people to go to Westminster Fair in the depth of winter; he enjoined the City to pay for the keep of his bear and his elephant—a small thing, but an invasion of the liberties; he instigated his servants to pick quarrels with the young citizens—and all of course was paid for by a new fine.

There is no need to follow the disputes of the King and the City during this unhappy time. The Mayors were deposed, and sent to prison; tallages, aids, and fines were constantly imposed. The King's Justices held courts within the walls; and charters were sold by the King, to be broken again whenever it seemed convenient.

Edward the First carried it with a high hand over the charters of the citizens. Yet he was not capricious. A strong king, he made his power felt; imposed fines, removed mayors, and seized the liberties; yet was respected. It would seem that the late troubles had resulted in a general lowering of trade morality, for stringent laws were passed in this reign, regulating the prices and customs of bakers, millers, hucksters, and other sellers of provisions. Yet the City in this reign obtained a valuable charter, which confirmed fully all their old privileges, and added certain new ones, namely— (1) That the Mayor-elect, in the absence of the King and Barons of the Exchequer from Westminster, is to be presented and admitted by the Constable of the Tower; (2) to be free from pannage (which seems to have been the right of the King to send swine to feed in their forests), from pontage (a duty for the maintenance of bridges), and of murage (a duty for the repair of walls of cities and strong places).

The unhappy reign of Edward the Second began with an act which promised no favour from the Crown—an attempt, namely, to tax the City at the

King's own pleasure, contrary to the charter. The Mayor and Aldermen were intimidated into buying off the clause for a thousand pounds. For some time the Crown continued favourably disposed towards the City, employing an army of London citizens for the reduction of Leeds Castle. In 1321, however, Edward seized the City's liberties; and, on the landing of the Queen with Prince Edward and the Hainaulters in September, 1322, he was rewarded by the defection of the City from his cause. Not only did the Londoners refuse to fight for the King, but they murdered the Bishop of Exeter, whom the King had appointed *custos* of the City, took possession of the Tower, dismissed the prisoners, and ill-treated the Chancellor so grievously that he died.

This conduct of the City was rewarded by Edward the Third with a charter which proved the most advantageous of any yet obtained by the citizens. It confirmed their ancient rights, and added the following privileges :—

The Mayor was to be one of the judges of *Oyer* and *Terminer*, for the trial of criminals in Newgate; the citizens were to have the right of " Infangtheft" and "Outfangtheft"—that is to say, they had the power of trying every thief taken (fan ed) within the city, and of reclaiming for trial, in one of their own courts, every thief taken without the city; they had a right to confiscate the goods of every criminal convicted in the city; they were allowed to devise in *mortmain,* a privilege which they nobly used in the foundation of the city charities; they could force foreign merchants to sell their goods within forty days of arrival, so that they might not hold them back in order to run up the price; the citizens were not to be chargeable with the support of those who took sanctuary; the office of Escheator was given to the Mayor; the citizens of London might hold courts of Pie Powder—that is to say, courts for the immediate despatch of quarrels and disputes—at the country fairs to which they took their wares; they were exempted from special tallages; their liberties were not to be stopped for any offence of their magistrates; merchandise was not to be rated by the King's officers; and there was to be no market within seven miles of London.

During the reign of Edward III., this charter remained inviolate; and the prosperity of the City would have proceeded by leaps and bounds, but for the dreadful pestilence of the year 1350—when, as is asserted, "scarce the tenth person of all sorts" was left alive—and the famine of the year 1359.

All their privileges pointed, of course, in one direction: the citizens wanted to manage their affairs—that is, to conduct their trade—for their own advantage, after their own fashion, and without interference from the King. The early history of London is the history of the long and watchful struggle during which these liberties were one by one secured. It was a struggle in which the City took everything, and gave back nothing. There were times when the royal power was stronger than their own: then they were quiet and conciliatory, paid fines, gave great gifts, entertained princes royally, courted the favour of the heir. They were generally on the winning side. They favoured Prince Edward in the Barons' war; they were Yorkists in the Wars of the Roses; they were Roundheads in Charles's war; they were Whigs in the Revolution of 1688. Little by little the City shook off the yoke of King and Bishop. All was not yet done when Whittington began his apprenticeship, because Richard the Second was coming, who would try to take away what his grandfathers had given ; but the City was already practically free : its liberties had been granted, and could always be claimed as a right ; the citizens owned allegiance to none but masters of their own election ; and in case of civil war, the most important thing for either party to consider was, the side which might be taken by the Londoners.   " In the city and neighbourhood," says Froissart, " there are 24,000 men, completely armed, and fully 30,000 archers.   This is a great force ; they are bold and courageous ; and the more blood is spilled, the greater is their courage."

SIR RICHARD WHITTINGTON.

CHAPTER I.

BIRTH AND BOYHOOD.

"What would you have me do?"
"Learn to be wise, and practise how to thrive."

WHEN one man out of a whole generation is selected by posterity as especially worthy to be remembered and had in honour, the choice seems to be influenced especially by that quality which we call force of character; the power, namely, which some men possess of impressing themselves strongly upon their contemporaries. Other successful merchants lived in London at the same time as Whittington; others filled the high and responsible office of Mayor as often, and with as much honour and credit; others received kings with as much dignity; others maintained the liberties of the city with as much determination; others were as charitable, as generous, as patriotic, and as prudent. Yet

Whittington outshone all the citizens of his time. He alone was regarded, even in his lifetime, as *flos mercatorum*, the flower of London merchants. To him alone, whether of the Worshipful Company and Mystery of Mercers, or of any other craft, it has been granted to become the pattern for all ambitious prentices, a shining example of how a penniless boy may rise to wealth and honour by the aid of certain virtues—industry, honesty, patience, thrift, and courage—which are as rare in these days as they were when Dick trudged along the muddy roads on his way to conquer Fortune. It will be the aim of this book to show, as nearly as may be gathered, by what kind of life, by what acts and deeds, and under what circumstances, Richard Whittington won this crown of honour.

We find the name written in various ways,[1] as happened to most names before spelling was exalted to one of the necessities of civilisation. In the matter of spelling, every man was then a law unto himself, so that those who thought that an *h* would improve the look of a word put one in, and while some were pleased with the severity of an *i*, others preferred the beauty of a *y*. It would be, however, mere pedantry

---

[1] Among these ways are the following :—Whitington, Whytington, Whityngton, Whittington, Whyttyngton, Wityndon, Whytindon, Witinton, Wittingdon, Wittington, and Wityngton.

to spell the name of Whittington in any other way than that sanctioned by custom.

As regards the time and place of Whittington's birth—his origin, his family, his circumstances—all these things remained in the uncertainty of legend and tradition until some twenty years ago, when the researches of a most patient and careful antiquary— the Rev. Samuel Lysons—finally settled the whole question beyond dispute. It had been previously maintained, without any proof for any single assertion, that Whittington was born at Taunton Dean, at Ellesmere in Shropshire, at some unknown town in Herefordshire, or in Lancashire, the only reason for the statement being some vague tradition or a similarity of name.

At first sight it would seem a hopeless task to discover the family of a man who came to London in the fourteenth century as a boy, and stayed there all his life. It was before the time of parish registers; the man's name is not uncommon. But there was one fact about Whittington, previously overlooked by his historians—who were not antiquaries, but tradition collectors and story-tellers; it was, that Whittington bore a coat of arms—not one granted him by the King as to a newly-risen man, but one to which he was entitled by birth. The coat is described in heraldic language as " Gules, a fesse componé, or and azure ; crest, a lion's head, erased sable, langgued gules." The crest was changed by Whittington from the lion's head to a bee, or May-fly, the wings tipped with gold. It was a time of universal symbolism—a symbolism readily interpreted by the people—so that the crests, the heraldic devices, the coats of arms, the shape and colour of banners and bannerets, the trappings of horses, the fantastic figures in a pageant, the accessories of punishment, the marshalling and order of a procession, were so many proclamations of rank, dignity, family history, rights, honours, or infamy, read and understood by those who looked on as clearly as is a printed book in modern times. By the bee (if it was a bee) Whittington probably symbolised, and was well understood as symbolising, the slow and patient toil by which success is obtained. The industrious apprentice would observe the symbol of the bee as the great merchant rode through the streets. It admonished him and encouraged him as clearly as if it had been a picture by Hogarth. If, on the other hand, the crest was meant to be a May-fly, with wings gold-tipped, perhaps the uncertainty and ephemeral nature of human happiness was indicated. Certainly in those days, even more than now, men did well to remember that plague, pestilence, and famine, battle, murder, and sudden death, are continually nigh and threatening. But, to my eyes, the crest looks more like a bee.

Now this coat of arms, with the lion's head for crest

instead of the bee, was borne by a family whose history has been clearly traced by Dr. Lysons. Early in the 13th century they held an estate "in Herefordshire, called Soler's Hope. Thence they migrated to the village of Pauntley, in Gloucestershire, where they acquired another estate, probably the greater of the two, or perhaps the more desirable as a place of residence.

"The village of Pauntley," says Dr. Lysons, "is at a considerable distance from any town of consequence, and can scarcely be called a village. It consists of the church and manor-house, which stand close to each other, and a few scattered houses here and there at a distance from the church. The whole present population is only 256, and doubtless was much smaller in Whittington's time. The church is a beautiful specimen of the early Norman. The zig-zag arch which separates the chancel from the body of the church is singularly fine, as also the arch of the south doorway. To the north is a very ancient porch, built of fine old English oak. There are still remains to be seen of the old manor-house, a portion of which is now used as an out-house and a dove-cot, in which there is a good semicircular-headed doorway. There is no parsonage at Pauntley. The living, which is valued at £80 per annum, is in the gift of the Bishop of Gloucester and Bristol. I could not help feeling a singular interest when I walked over the ground on which Whittington had trod—sat in the church porch where he had probably sat—and entered the church in which he had worshipped as a boy, and in which, doubtless, he was baptised. The Abbey of Cormeilles, in Normandy, one of the alien priories, had a priory in the parish, and also had the advowson of Pauntley (Henry II.), which remained in their possession until the dissolution of the monasteries, when it was granted to Sir Giles Pole, who married Elizabeth, the youngest of the co-heiresses of Thomas Whittington, the last male of the direct branch of the family. By the will of Robert Whittington (1424), it appears that Pauntley was the burial-place of the family. He desires to be buried in the Church of St. John the Evangelist, in Pauntley. His son Guy, by will (1440), desires to be buried in the New Chapel of St. George in the above church, which marks the date and name of that which is now the south aisle. The church itself seems to have been built soon after the Conquest, probably by Walter de Pauntley.

"A second visit to Pauntley, in July 10th, 1860, brought to light circumstances connected with the history of the Whittington family overlooked on the occasion of the first visit, which bear peculiarly on the confirmation of the family pedigree. In the north window of the chancel still exist the remains of ancient stained glass, on which are emblazoned the arms of Whittington, with those of the Linets, Stauntons, and Peresfords, families with whom the Whittingtons intermarried; while in the west window, under the tower, are found the arms of Whittington impaling Melbourne on the right hand side, and on the left those of Whittington impaling Fitz-Warren, thus clearly identifying our hero, whose wife was Alice Fitz-Warren, with the Pauntley family beyond dispute."

The head of the family in the year 1350 was Sir William Whittington, whose age is unknown, but he was at the time unmarried. He married, either in 1352 or 1353, probably the latter, the widow of Sir Thomas de Berkeley, a member of the great House of that name, of Coverley, in Gloucestershire. Sir Thomas died in 1352, leaving his widow as a jointure the estate of Stoke Orchard. Three sons (Dr. Lyson says " perhaps " five children, but gives no reason) were the fruit of the second marriage. It is important, therefore, to bear in mind that the ordinary ideas about Whittington's origin are groundless. He was not friendless, nor was he of obscure origin. He was of gentle birth: his father was a knight and a county squire : his mother belonged to the family of Mansel, a Devonshire house of the same rank : his half-brothers, if he had any, were of the house of Berkeley. Such advantages, therefore, as good birth could bestow upon a lad were his. He came of a good old stock, and was neither a country clown nor gutter-born town lad.

Somewhere about the year 1358, Sir William Whittington was outlawed ; it is not known for what offence, but it is conjectured by Dr. Lyson that it was the marrying of Sir Thomas Berkeley's widow without the royal consent, and he adduces examples of outlawry for this offence. He died in outlawry in the year 1360. We may therefore place the birth of Richard Whittington, who was the youngest, about the year 1358.

The three boys thus left without a father at a tender age were named respectively William, Robert, and Richard. The estate of Pauntley became the jointure of Dame Whittington, who thus possessed for life two estates, and could not have been badly off. The eldest, who took Soler's Hope, and eventually Pauntley, grew to manhood, and married one Catherine Staunton, but died without children; whereupon the estates went to the second brother Robert, who also married and had issue, one of his sons, Guy, being present at the field of Agincourt. His descendants occupied the estate for nearly two hundred years. A branch of the family still exists at the village of Hamswill, in the parish of Cold Ashton, not many miles from Pauntley; and many persons of the name claim to be descended from this brother of Sir Richard.

The Whittingtons, then, were of a good old race, and lived on their own lands, which were farmed for them by three *villains*. The estate would yield enough and to spare of corn and grain, cider and mead, hay and grass, cattle, sheep, and bacon for their own use; while the woodland, which then formed so large a part of every country estate, was hunted over by the sons of the house for venison and game.

As for education in a country village, there were but two ways possible. If the family was not rich enough to secure the services of a clerk as private tutor, the parson of the parish had to undertake the task, no doubt in accordance with the Solomonic method, so that the boys could cry out, like him of the song—

> " I wold fayne be a clarke,
> But yet hit is a strange werke;
> The birchen twiggis be so sharpe,
> Hit makyth me have a faynt harte.
> What availeth it me though I say nay?
>
> " I wold my master were an hare.
> And all his bokis howndis were,
> And I myself a joly huntere;
> To blow my horn I wold not spare;
> For if he were dede I coold not care."

Many boys of good family were put into great houses, where they became " Henxmen," or " Bele Babies," and were taught to ride, to bear armour, to learn courtesy in speech and deed, reading, singing, harping, dancing, languages, and other useful things. But these lads were not designed for the city. Where a priest could not be found for a private house, a boy might be sent to one of the great convents, where the abbots received a limited number of boys. There were no grammar schools in the country to which a Gloucestershire boy might conveniently be sent. Hereford school was founded in 1384, too late for the Whittingtons.

It is hard to understand how younger sons in those days got settled in the world. Probably a good many, especially on great estates, remained in the castle or manor-house acting as stewards, managers, or bailiffs; they might look forward, after a period of service, to taking up farms and small estates bought for them; and they would marry girls whose dowry would be in land. Some would go into the Church; but it must be remembered that, though we find Henry the Fifth's uncle a Bishop of Winchester and a Courtenay the Bishop of London, in the fourteenth century respect for ecclesiastics was small, while the facilities of the convent school opened the door to the rise of poor and humble boys of ability. " Every cobbler's son," says Piers Plowman, " is becoming a clerk first and then a bishop, and great lords have to bow down before him." The Church was the one profession by which a lad of ignoble birth could rise to eminence; and in proportion as the sons of peasants thronged into it, the better classes kept aloof. The ranks of the Church, in Whittington's time, were recruited in much the same way as they are now in Ireland, France, and Belgium, where the Church is handed over to the peasant class, to whom it is a life-long joy that their sons should say mass in all the pomp and splendour of the Roman ritual. But youths of gentle blood, unless irresistibly impelled by the love of learning, or urged by the prospect of gaining one of the great offices of the Church, would not be tempted to take Holy Orders. If they could not stay at home, however, what could they do? They might enter the service of one of those great lords whose power lasted till the Wars of the Roses. They would act as pages and companions; they would learn manly exercises and the use of arms; they would practise in the tilt-yard, follow in the hunt, in case of war accompany their master and fight at his side. They would be dependants, but service was honourable and safe. The livery of a great lord ensured a maintenance; dinner and supper were spread in the great hall at the common board for all; horse and arms were provided; perhaps, after loyal service, a daughter of the house was given to wife, and an estate on which to sit down and found another branch of the family.

Suppose, however, that a lad had no taste for the

vie bruyante, the noisy, loud, and rough life of a great lord's service, what else could he do ? The Law was open to him ; he might become a student of one of the Inns of Court. Here he would find none but such as, like himself, were of good family, with many who studied law as the education most suited for the life of a country gentleman. We may remember—because the happy continuity of English life and manners renders such a parallel possible—that Justice Shallow was in his youth a student of law. Other professions there were none. The barbers were surgeons, and let blood ; there were no engineers, architects, bankers, or writers ; there was no army in which to hold a commission ; there was no standing navy ; there was no Civil Service, unless a post in the Royal Household might be called a Civil Service ; there was only one way possible outside service, the church, or the law by which a lad could earn his livelihood, which was by practising some honourable trade or mystery in a great city.

It must not be imagined that these prentices of the City of London were of mean and humble origin ; not at all. The sons of freemen of the City, or boys of good and honourable families, alone were admitted to the seven years of apprenticeship. The common people, the *ascripti glebæ*—the poor rustics who were bound to the soil, and could not leave their native fields—had no part or share in the fortunes of the City of London. Many of the burgesses were proud of their descent as well as of their liberties; and if they were, as Froissart calls them, a presumptuous folk, they were in many cases actual cousins by blood of the knights and lords who were jealous of their freedom. So that, when we read of noble families descended from city worthies, it is well to remember that most likely their very founders were themselves of gentle descent.

One or two additional facts have been collected about the Whittington family. The "inlawry" was accomplished after Sir William's death, perhaps at some expense in way of fines—a fact which Dr. Lysons brings to bear upon his theory of Whittington's early life.

He was, he says, the youngest son of an honourable but impoverished house. His mother married again, and had a second family. This is a mistake, because, as already stated, Sir William Whittington was her second husband, and not Sir Thomas Berkeley. He goes on to build up a story about neglect, ill-treatment by his elder brothers (who were only a year or two older than himself), and final resolution to run away and seek his fortune in London. He might have gone to Gloucester, but it was too near to Pauntley (says Dr. Lysons), and would probably have reminded him of his own family, and their treatment of him; he would desire to get away as far as possible; he would put the whole breadth of England between himself and his mother.

All this is pure imagination, with not a single fact to rest upon. I read the story very differently. I find a country lad, the youngest of three : his eldest brother succeeds to the property ; the second stays on the estate. The third shall be sent to London, and apprenticed, not to a handicraft, but to an honourable trade ; not to a meanly born tradesman, but to a man of good old west-country stock, known well to all the Whittingtons, Berkeleys, and Mansels. To him the boy shall be sent ; he has promised to receive him into his service. He will take care that the slender portion of the youngest son shall not be wasted ; he will teach the boy the mystery of buying and selling ; he will launch him into the great world.

As regards the boy's animosity towards his own kin, it is clearly disproved by the facts that he placed his arms in the church of Pauntley, that he ordered prayers for the souls of his father and mother, and that he left a valuable collection of plate to his brother.

At the age of thirteen, then, and somewhere about the year 1371, the lad was sent up to London to seek his fortune in the usual way, by apprenticeship and honourable trade.

As for the way from Gloucester to London, roads,

like streets, never change if they are left to themselves. Country people follow the same track as
their fathers, without considering whether the lie
of the land would perhaps admit of an easier or a
straighter way; inns and refreshment houses spring
up, which make change more difficult; so that,
though the broad highway has taken the place of the
bridle-path, he who would ride from Pauntley to
London would now ride by much the same road as
that followed by little Dick Whittington, who probably
walked all the way, without feeling that method of
travel a hardship at all.

There was a great deal of traffic between the quiet
west country and London in those days; there was
the sending up, on pack-horses, of wool, and the
bringing back of silks, broadcloths, spices, scented
woods, wines, and all the things which could be got
in London. Nothing could be sent down to the
country except on the backs of horses; there were no
waggons, coaches, canals, or boats. Sometimes the
drivers brought back their beasts laden; sometimes
they returned with the produce in marks, shillings,
and silver pence, carrying the money in leathern
purses tied to their girdles. They went up to town,
and they returned, in strong companies; and all were
armed, for there were robbers lurking near every
wood. They carried or bought their own provisions
on the way, for at the inns they found nothing but

sleeping accommodation, and that of the roughest, with two or three in a bed. They carried their valuables to their sleeping-rooms with them, or kept watch over them all night. On the march, they looked suspiciously, weapon in hand, at every coppice of trees or clump of tangled brier and brushwood, because behind it there might be lurking some band of desperate villains, hoping to rush upon them unawares, to kill and plunder. A shame that roads should be left thus grown over! And yet a law was passed by King Edward the First, that all roads, in those places where woods, bushes, and dykes are found, in which wicked men may find a hiding-place, should be enlarged to a width of twenty feet on either hand, great trees only excepted. There is a piece of road on the way from Upton-on-Severn to Tewkesbury, in this same county of Gloucestershire, which may remind the traveller of the bridle-path along which these long caravans of beasts laden with wool and flax slowly moved. It is a made road now, but it was then a narrow track, and on either side stretches the flat and wooded heath, where an army of robbers might hide themselves. It has a cold and suspicious look; the trees are noble, but between them lies, in parts, the thick and treacherous underwood. As that road is now, so were all the roads in Gloucestershire in those days, when, for every hundred acres of cleared land, there were a thousand of woodland **chase and** forest.

The condition of the country is shown by **the** singular adventure which happened, some years later, to Robert Whittington, Squire of **Pauntley.** He was riding near Hereford with his son Guy— perhaps they had been to look at the family estate of Soler's Hope—when they were suddenly attacked by a band of robbers, thirty in all, among whom were eight of the household of Richard Oldcastle, a gentle- man of the county. Resistance was useless, and they were carried off to Dynmore Hill, where they were robbed, and kept all night in a deserted chapel. Next day they were informed that they would be either put to death, or taken across the March into Wales—a fate which they seem to have considered as worse, on the whole, than being killed, though one does not see why—unless they could procure ransom. Guy was allowed to go, in order to make some arrangements for the raising of the sum demanded. When he returned, offering a substantial sum, the two prisoners, father and son, were released, after solemnly swearing to pay £600 for ransom, and to forego all actions or prosecutions for their imprison- ment. They came away, and immediately supplicated the King to declare such a covenant, entered into with the knife at their throats, null and void ; so that they paid none of the money. It is not apparent what became of the robbers, or if any of them were brought to justice. It may, however, be remarked that Sir Robert Whittington, whatever his father's circumstances were, must have been a man of very considerable substance, to be ransomed at what was then an enormous sum of money.

Richard was doubtless sent to London under the escort of a caravan of wool-carriers ; he would perform the journey in five or six days, and one hopes that he had no more unpleasant experience on the way than a scare now and then, when ill-favoured ones, too few to venture on an attack, scowled upon the band of carriers from the depths of the forest. He marched along the bridle-path which we now call Oxford Street, and he entered the City of the Golden Pavement by that gate which he afterwards cleansed, purified, and rebuilt—the gate where so many criminals have waited in anguish for the end. To enter by way of Newgate might have been a bad omen ; but the boy was thinking not of omens, but of his future life, and of Sir John Fitz-Warren, who was to be his master.

CHAPTER II.

THE CITY OF LONDON.

"City of ancient memories! Thy spires
Rise o'er the dust of worthy sons; thy walls,
Within their narrow compass, hold as much
Of Freedom as the whole wide world beside."

A SURVEY OF LONDON for the fourteenth century does not, unhappily, exist. Yet an abundance of light is thrown upon the City, its walls, castles, its churches, streets, and great houses, in the pages of *Liber Albus*, Walsingham, Riley's "Memorials," Froissart, Chaucer, Lydgate, and other authorities, and it is easy to construct a survey of the City with almost as much accuracy as that of Stow.

To begin with, it occupied very much the same space as that now covered by the City proper; its streets were narrow and winding, yet there were still left many open spaces; it was crowded with people; its river was full of shipping; it was rich, prosperous, and, as we shall presently see, possessed of a considerable amount of liberty.

The great wall of London, broad and strong, with towers at intervals, was two miles and 608 feet long from end to end, beginning at the Tower of London on the east, and ending at the Fleet River and the Thames on the west. It was originally surrounded by a moat or ditch 200 feet broad, which was finished in the year 1213. But the ditch speedily became the receptacle for all the city rubbish which could not be thrown into the river, and in the course of a hundred and fifty years it was completely choked and filled up, being, no doubt, one of the causes of the many dreadful pestilences which fell upon the City. It was cleaned out and repaired by the direction of John Philpot, Mayor, in the year 1379, and eight years later it was ordered to be kept in repair by means of a toll. During the time, then, with which we are most concerned, the moat was a broad and clear piece of water running round the whole north of the City, crossed by bridges and causeways here and there. In Stow's time—that is, before the end of Queen Elizabeth's reign—it was almost entirely filled up, planted with gardens, and with houses built upon the banks.

As regards the gates, there were anciently only four—namely, Aldgate, Aldersgate, Ludgate, and Bridgegate—that is to say, one for each of the cardinal points. Then other gates and posterns were added for the convenience of the citizens: Bishop-

The Tower of London.

gate, for those who had business in the direction of Norfolk, Suffolk, or Cambridgeshire; Moorgate, for those who would practise archery, or take their recreation in Moor Fields; Cripplegate, more ancient than the two preceding, had a prison for debtors attached to it; and there was also a postern for the convent of Grey Friars, now Christ's Hospital. At Newgate was a small, incommodious, and fever-haunted prison for criminals, whose wretched condition moved the compassion of Walworth first and Whittington next. And at Ludgate was another prison, appropriated to debtors, trespassers, and those who committed contempt of court.

Along the river side were several water-gates, the chief of which were Blackfriars, Queenhithe, Dowgate, and Billingsgate. These, like the gates to the north wall, were ordered to be diligently guarded by night, " for fear of French deceits."

> " Per noctem portæ clauduntur Londiniarum.
> Mœnia ne forte fraus frangat Francigenarum."

The citizens of the fourteenth century regarded the lordly Tower of London with fear and jealousy rather than pride, because it represented the royal pretensions against which they were continually struggling in the maintenance of their liberties. It was a standing menace; and it was associated with the death of those who had fallen in the battle of

freedom. The early reformers, who attempted too
much, and were hanged, beheaded, and quartered
as seditious and pestilent fellows, instead of being
honoured as patriots, chiefly met their doom in the
Tower—Fitz-Osbert in 1196, Constantine Fitz-Arnulph
in 1222, the Sheriffs in 1253, the Mayor, Aldermen,
and Sheriffs in 1265, for instance. The Tower was
the citadel for the defence of the town ; it was also
a State prison ; it was a royal residence ; it was the
Mint ; it was the Armoury ; it was the treasury of
the ornaments and jewels of the Crown ; it was the
principal Record Office ; and it was, besides, the
place from which the King could form a point of
vantage, assail the privileges and liberties of the City,
by demanding toll, tithe, and tallage in the teeth of
old and hardly-won Royal Charters.

The following story illustrates the popular feeling
towards the Tower :—

King Henry III. had built a noble tower, with
portal, walls, and bulwarks, for the adornment and
strengthening of the Tower. Hardly were the works
completed than, on the night of St. George, the foundations gave way, and the whole fell to the ground.
The work was again taken in hand, and the tower
rebuilt. Again it fell to the ground. Now there
was a certain priest in London, to whom, in a dream,
there appeared the venerable figure of an archbishop
bearing a cross in his hand. He advanced to the

newly-built walls, regarded them with a stern and
threatening aspect, and struck them with his cross,
whereupon they all fell to the ground. The sleeping
priest, in his dream, asked an attendant on the archbishop what might be the meaning of this, and was
answered that he saw before him the sainted Thomas
a Becket, son of Gilbert, Portreeve of London, who
overturned these walls because he knew them to be
designed for the injury and prejudice of the Londoners, whom he loved, and not for defence of the
kingdom.

Within the narrow space of the city walls there
rose a forest of towers and spires. The piety of
merchants had erected no fewer than a hundred and
three churches, which successive citizens were continually rebuilding, beautifying, or enlarging. They
were filled with the effigies and splendid tombs, the
painted and gilded arms, of their founders and benefactors, for whose souls masses were continually said.
It was a time when religious ceremonies attended
every act of official life. On seven days in the year
the Mayor heard mass at St. Paul's, attended by the
sheriffs, aldermen, and the liveries. Every Company
had its own church or chapel. Besides the parish
churches, there were many splendid churches belonging to the priories and monasteries. Foremost among
them was the great church of St. Paul. It was begun
to be built, after the burning of the old church in the

year 1087, by Maurice, Bishop of London, and the
work was carried on by his successors, who enclosed
the cathedral on the north and south sides by a strong
wall and gates, with what object is not apparent.
The building was continued through the whole of the
twelfth century, the steeple being finished in the year
1222. The church, when finished, was 720 feet long,
the breadth was 130 feet, and the height was 150 feet.
It is shown in Agas's "View of London" (*temp.*
Elizabeth) as a great church, cruciform, with a tower,
but no steeple. On the north side was a cloister,
surrounding a plot of ground called Pardon Churchyard, and painted (but this was after the death of
Whittington) with a Dance of Death, like the ceme-
tery of St. Innocents in Paris; on the same side also
were a College of Petty Canons, founded by Richard
II., and a chapel of the Holy Ghost; under the choir
was the Jesus Chapel; and at the west end of this
chapel, also under the choir, was the parish church of
St. Faith. Again, on the north side was a charnel-
house for the bones of the dead, and over it a chapel.
On the east side stood a high bell-tower, square, built
of stone, containing four bells, and covered with a
leaden spire, in which was an image of St. Paul. In
the midst of the churchyard was the famous pulpit-
cross of timber, mounted upon steps of stone, from
which sermons were read, bulls proclaimed, and other
functions performed. The church itself, which

resembled Winchester Cathedral in many of its
features, was filled with monuments of dead worthies,
among whom were, according to Stow—Kings Seba,
of the East Saxons, and Etheldred, of the West
Saxons; many of the Bishops of London; the deans,
chancellors, canons, and prebends of the cathedral;
John of Gaunt, Duke of Lancaster, with Blanche, his
first wife; Sir Richard Burley, Knight of the Garter;
and a vast number of deceased city worthies—mayors,
aldermen, and great merchants. The monuments of
the church were numerous, but they were not to be
compared with those in the churches of the Grey
Friars and the Black Friars, the reason being the
universal desire to be buried in the company of holy
men.

The City, at the close of the fourteenth century, was
much richer in great and noble houses than it is at
present. Not one of the houses, great or small, of
Whittington's youth now remain, the oldest of the
ancient City buildings, the Guildhall and Crosby Hall,
being of fifteenth-century time. The most important
was perhaps Baynard's Castle, the name of which
still survives to mark the spot on which it stood on
the bank of the river, close to Blackfriars Bridge.
This place belonged to the hereditary bearers of the
City banner, the Fitz-Walters, from the year 1216 to
the end of the following century. The castle was
greatly damaged by fire in the year 1428, after which

D

it was rebuilt by Humphrey, Duke of Gloucester.
Henry VII. repaired it, and made it his own residence.
It was here that the Council was held which resolved
upon proclaiming Queen Mary. In the time of
Elizabeth it belonged to the Earl of Pembroke; and
it was finally destroyed in the Great Fire, being then
the residence of the Earls of Shrewsbury.

Close to Baynard's Castle, on the west, had formerly
stood the Tower of Mountfiquit, but this was taken
down in the year 1276 to make room for the Church
of the Black Friars; and still farther west, at the end
of the City wall, on the banks of the Thames, stood
another tower, built and kept repaired at the charges
of the City. Beyond Fleet River, outside the wall,
had formerly stood a tower on the spot where Bridewell was afterwards erected. The stones were used
in the rebuilding of St. Paul's after the fire of the
year 1087. The house remained, and was used by
King John for a Parliament, but in Whittington's
time it was an open space, used as a "lay stall," or
place for the throwing of refuse and rubbish. It was
rebuilt much later by Henry VIII.

The name of the Barbican preserves the memory of
a watch-tower which formerly stood there, without
the City wall. There were, however, other Barbicans,
especially those erected by the Barons in the war
with Henry III.

The great Tower Royal, which stood in the street

still called after it, was an old and historical place
even in the time of Whittington. It was called
by Edward III. his Inn, named the Royal, and
was given by him to his college of St. Stephen at
Westminster. In the reign of Richard II. the
Crown had recovered it, for it was then known
as the Queen's Wardrobe, where Richard's mother
remained during the Wat Tyler rebellion ; and in
the year 1386 the King received there "Lion,
King of Armonie," who had been chased out of his
realm by the Tartarians. It was subsequently turned
into a royal stable, and, in Stow's time, had been
divided into tenements and let out to divers men.

Another "King's house" was in Bucklersbury,
called "Serne's Tower." Among the more important
of the great houses may be mentioned, in Thames
Street, the place known as Cold Herbergh (Cold
Harbour) House. This house, after belonging to
several private citizens in succession, passed into the
hands of the Earl of Hereford, and from him to John
Holland, Earl of Huntingdon, brother to Richard the
Second. It was otherwise called Poultney's Inn,
after Sir John Poultney, four times Mayor, one of its
early owners. Henry the Fifth had it when Prince
of Wales. It was granted by Richard III. to Garter
King-at-Arms for a college of heralds, but it passed
out of their hands and fell into the possession of the
Earls of Shrewsbury, by whom it was ultimately

pulled down, and small houses erected in its place. In this street there were also many good houses belonging to merchants. In Fenchurch Street the Earls of Northumberland had a house; Leadenhall, which became the property of the citizens in the year 1408, and was a granary for storing corn against a time of dearth; there were the halls of the City Companies. On Cornhill stood the "Tun" Prison (so called because in shape it resembled a cask), until the year 1401, when it was pulled down, and a conduit of water brought from Tyburn took its place; on the north side of Cornhill was the "Weigh" House, where foreign merchandise was weighed at the "King's Beam;" in Eastcheap was the great house called the "Garland." On Fish Street Hill was the old palace of Edward the Black Prince, afterwards converted into an inn; in St. Michael's Lane was the "Leaden Porch," also converted afterwards into an inn; in Walbrook was the Stocks Market, called after the stocks, which stood hard by—it was one of the five markets erected for the sale of fish and flesh, the others being Bridge Street, East Chepe, Old Fish Street, and St. Nicolas' shambles. Wool was weighed in the churchyard of St. Mary Wool Church, next to this market. In Dowgate stood Jesus' College, a society of priests, with a library. Here were also two famous old houses, named Erber and the Old Hall; close by was the Steel-yard. This place was the quarter inhabited by the Hanseatic merchants. The origin of this remarkable mercantile colony was very ancient. They obtained a settlement in London before the Conquest, and were known as the *Guilda Aula Teutonicorum.* They obtained charters from successive kings, with confirmation of their privileges and rights of trade. They might elect their alderman, and import their merchandise, which they were ordered to sell within forty days unless expressly forbidden for special reasons. Their liberty was seized by Edward VI., on complaint of the English merchants. They imported grain, ropes, masts, pitch, tar, flax, hemp, linen cloth, wax, steel, and other things.

Near the Tower Royal stood Ypres Inn, named after its builder, William of Ypres, a Fleming of King Stephen's reign. Here, in the tumult of the year 1377, the seditious citizens tried to lay hands upon the Duke of Lancaster and the Marshal, who escaped by flight. In Basinghall Street was Bakewell Hall, one of the most ancient of the City houses, where was held a weekly market ; and it was ordered by Whittington, in the first of his three years of office, that no foreigner should sell woollen cloth but in Bakewell Hall. In Basing Lane was another ancient house, called, later, Gerrard's Hall, after a supposed giant so called, whose staff, a great fir pole forty feet long, and ladder, were shown to visitors. But Stow

has shown that the hall was formerly called after Sir
John Gisors, its owner, and that the staff was nothing
but an old Maypole, and the ladder that which was
employed to decorate it.   Guildhall stood somewhat
west of the present site, on which the new Guildhall
was commenced in the year 1411.   Beside it stood
the Chapel or College of St. Magdalen, now incorporated with St. Lawrence Jewry, called also London
College.   It possessed a library, for which a new
building was erected, in conformity with the terms of
Whittington's will.   In the Jewry stood the old
synagogue which had belonged to the Jews before
their expulsion in 1291 ; an order of monks, called
Fratres de Penitentia Jesu, turned it into a chapel.
The real centre of the city seems to have been Chepe.
Here, or close by, were St. Paul's Cathedral and Bow
Church ; here was the Hospital of St. Thomas Acon ;
here was the " Standard " of Chepe, which contained
the great conduit.   It was at the Standard, and over
against the place where the mercers had their shops,
that executions of citizens, especially those of the
hasty and tumultuous kind, took place.   Whittington
may have witnessed here the beheadal of Sheriff
Richard Lions by Wat Tyler in 1381 ; but most
likely, on that day of rebuke and anarchy, he was
with his Company, preparing for the defence of the
city.   In Chepe was the great Cross, the last but one
of those erected by Edward the First to mark the

place where rested the body of his Queen on the way
to Westminster. At the west end was another cross,
taken down in the year 1390. On the west of Bow
Church was a stone gallery, erected by Edward III.
for witnessing tournaments; and, beyond, an open
space called the Meadow, where the mercers had
their shops. This was the heart of the City and the
centre of trade. All the pageants, processions, riotings,
and "chevauchés" passed along Chepe; in its broad
road knights rode in tilt on great days; on ordinary
days the stalls round the Standard were crowded with
buyers, the citizens thronged about the booths, men-
at-arms rode up and down, kings' purveyors walked,
carrying wands of office, from shop to shop, prisoners
were carried to the pillory preceded by fife and drum;
from time to time a quarrel arose, with brandishing of
knives and clash of steel; the prentices shouted at
their booths; the great City ladies walked about
rustling in silk and satin, with gold chains and scarlet
wimples; their humbler sisters vied with them in
brave attire; the men went clad as gorgeously as
the women. It was a time of splendid dress and costly
adornment; personal property took the form of gold
and silver cups, hoods broidered with pearls, robes
and gowns of bright colour and great price.

The water supply of the City was formerly derived
from the brooks and streams that flowed through it,
and the wells which stood within and without the

walls. The river of Wells, called afterwards the Fleet Ditch; the Walbrook, which ran through the midst of the city; and a bourn which ran through Langbourn Ward, furnished an ample supply of water in early times. When these water-courses became corrupted within the walls by things thrown in, the citizens had recourse to the streams outside the town, the principal of which was Holborn or Oldborne stream, which fell into the Wells river, where is now the Holborn Viaduct. The principal wells were Holy Well, Clement's Well, and Clark's or Clerken Well, at the west end of Clerkenwell Church. In the year 1236 water was brought from Tyburn in leaden conduits, and, fifty years later, from Paddington, to the City. The " Standard " of Chepe was the great place for the drawing of water. Later on, as we shall see, Whittington provided the first drinking fountains, in the form of " bosses," put up in various places.

The City has always been well provided with hospitals. Those in the fourteenth century were St. Katherine's, by the Tower; St. Anthony's, with a free school; St. Bartholomew's; St. Giles in the Fields, founded by the Queen of Henry I. for lepers; St. John of Jerusalem; St. James in the Field, also for lepers; St. Mary's, within Cripplegate, founded by William Elsing, Mercer, in the year 1332; St. Mary of Bethlehem; St. Mary without Bishopsgate; St. Mary Rouncevall, by Charing Cross; St. Thomas of

Acon in Chepe, which afterwards became the Mercers' Chapel; and others.

These were the principal monuments of the great City. Its residents were not all merchants and craftsmen; besides a large number of priests, friars, and monks, there were a good number of houses, as we have seen, belonging to great nobles, but of course the great mass of the people were those occupied with its commerce and industries. And such was the close and jealous guarding of the trades, so strictly were the crafts ruled and administered, such was the protection, that, naturally, those of the same calling gathered together in and about the same streets, where the overseers could easily take care that none should undersell the other, nor any expose for sale goods of inferior quality and make. For the English reputation for honesty and good work was not a plant of spontaneous growth, but was the work of many generations of wise and thoughtful rulers. Thus the mercers, in the time of which we write, kept their shops in Cheapside, as in the *London Lackpenny:*—

> " Then to the Chepe I began me drawne,
> Where much people I saw for to stande;
> One offered me velvet, sylke, and lawne,
> Another he takethe me by the hande—
> ' Here is Paris thred, the fynest in the lande.' "

The goldsmiths occupied Guthrun's Lane—now Gutter Lane, in which will still be found Goldsmith

Street ; the pepperers and grocers in Soper's Lane—
which is now gone. They migrated from that part
to Bucklersbury, most of which is also gone. The
drapers were found in Lombard Street and Cornhill;
the skinners, in St. Mary Pellipers and St. Mary
Axe ; the pelterers, in Walbrook, Cornhill, and
Budge Row ;[1] the stock fishmongers, in Thames
Street ; the " wet " fishmongers, in Knightrider
Street and Bridge Street ; the ironmongers, in
Ironmongers' Lane and Old Jewry : the vintners,
in the Vintry ; the brewers, along the river side ;
the butchers, in Eastcheap, St. Nicolas' Shambles,
and the Stock Market ; the hosiers, in Hosier Lane ;
the shoemakers, in Cordwayner street ; the founders,
in Lothbury ; the cooks, in Thames Street and East
Chepe. Lydgate says :—

> " Then I hyed me unto East Chepe ;
>   One cryes ' Ribbs of beef and many **a** pye !'
> Pewter pottes they clattered in a heape ;
>   There was harpe, pype, and mynstrelsye."

Poulters frequented the Poultry ; paternoster-makers
and makers of beads for prayers were found in
Paternoster Row ; and so on, the names of the streets

---

[1] In the Ordinances of the Pelterers (Riley's " Memorials," p. 330)
it is enacted that the freemen of the trade shall dwell in Walbrook,
Cornhill, and Budge Row, and not in other " foreign " streets in the
City, " that so the overseers of the trade may be able to oversee them."

themselves being an indication of their earliest inhabitants.

Such was the City of London as Whittington saw it. We must imagine a small compact town, enclosed by a wall two miles and a quarter in length ; a town smaller, for instance, in area than the modern Jerusalem—smaller than Hyde Park. Within are narrow winding streets, in which the people are more crowded than in any Edinburgh wynd. Many of these narrow lanes have sunlight and air shut out by great projections known as " halpaces" built out over them in order to give the houses larger rooms. All houses, both large and small, to prevent fire, are ordered to be built of stone up to a certain height, and their roofs were to be constructed of baked tiles—a wise ordinance, which should never have been allowed to fall into abeyance. There is no pavement in the streets, and they are not kept clean : there is no lighting at night : there is no service of scavengers ; everybody throws his refuse where he pleases—in the streets, on the river bank, in the city moat ; here it lies, and fills the air with noisome stenches. There is no water "laid on" in the house. The rich merchants' residences are great inns, standing four-square round a court, like the houses in France. Outside, they are rich with painted crests and coats of arms, glorious carving in black timber, and picturesque gables. Within, the rooms are dark and low

but every large house has one great hall, where the
sunlight, through painted windows, falls upon rich
tapestry bright with colour ; on robes of many hues,
edged with precious fur and set with pearls ; on gold
chains of office ; on sideboards covered with goblets
and plate of gold, of silver gilt, and parcel gilt, and
plain silver. Yet the air is heavy, and the rooms
want ventilation. The London citizen sits ever in
fear of plague, and knows not yet that the only
safeguard is to keep house and city and people clean.
Death is still before his eyes ; in the prisons hard by
the criminals perish daily of gaol fever ; life, which is
uncertain at the best, and can never be anything but
fleeting and transitory, seemed, and was, far more
uncertain in the fourteenth century than the nineteenth. Such was the town. We shall see presently
what manner of life they led, those merchants and
their prentices.

Without the walls, there were already, in the fourteenth century, especially on the west side, many
remarkable buildings. As Fitz-Stephen described
the suburbs in the twelfth century, so they were, little
altered, in the fourteenth. "On all sides," he says,
"without the houses of the suburbs, are the citizens'
gardens and orchards, planted with trees, large,
sightly, and adjoining together. On the north side
are pastures and plain meadows, with brooks running
through them, turning water-mills with a pleasant

rush. Not far off is a great forest"—he means
Hornsey Wood, probably, or Epping and Hainault
Forests—" a wild wooded chase, having good covert
for harts, bucks, does, boars, and wild bulls."

Outside the Tower, on the east, was St. Katherine's
Hospital. There were no buildings at all between this
and Wapping, the deserted river bank being a haunted
and dismal stretch, used for the hanging of pirates
and sea rovers. North-east of the town, Edward the
Third had founded, in the fields, an abbey called Grace
Abbey, and without Bishopsgate was the Hospital of
St. Mary of Bethlehem. These were all the buildings
in the east. The Moor, afterwards Moorfields, was a
broad flat, a neglected and marshy swamp, until
Henry V., in the year 1415, opened a postern in the
city wall, and made a causeway by which the citizens
could walk for recreation towards Islington and
Hoxton. Then it was cut across by dykes, which
drained it, and planted with gardens, trees, and wind-
mills. Beyond Smithfield was the Monastery of the
Charter-house, built on the place which Sir Walter
Manny, in the year 1349, purchased as a burial-place
for the thousands of poor creatures who died of the
plague. Here, also, was the Priory of St. John of
Jerusalem. On the west side—in Chancery Lane—
were the remains of the old Temple, built by the
Templars before they took up their more convenient
and more splendid quarters on the river. In the

same street were the house and gardens built by Ralph Nevil, Bishop of Chichester in the reign of Henry III. Here was also the House of " Converts " —*i.e.*, those Jews who pretended conversion to avoid expulsion ; it was appropriated by Edward III. for the use of the Master of the Rolls, the converted Jews having by that time died off or relapsed. The Church and House of the Preaching Friars *(Fratres Prædicatores*—they were Black Friars and Dominicans) stood also in Chancery Lane. Lincoln's Inn was built by the Earl of Lincoln about the year 1300, partly on the site of Bishop Nevil's garden, and partly on the site of the Preaching Friars' Priory, when they exchanged their abode for a more commodious one.

In Fleet Street there were standing, among the gardens and trees, Clifford's Inn, Sergeant's Inn, the ruins of the house afterwards called Bridewell, the Bishop of Salisbury's Inn, the Church and Priory of the White Friars *(fratres beatæ Mariæ de Monte Carmeli)*, and the Temple, lately granted by the Knights Hospitallers to the Students of the Common Law of England.

In the Strand were Exeter House, on the north, the Bishop of Bath's Inn, where Arundel House afterwards stood, the Bishop of Llandaff's house, the Bishop of Chester's house, the Bishop of Worcester's Inn (the last two on the site of Somerset House), the great Palace or House of Savoy, built in 1245, and destroyed by fire in 1381 by the rebels,[1] the Bishop of Carlisle's Inn, the King's Mews at Charing Cross, the Bishop of Norwich's house, the Hospital of St. Mary Rouncevall, and the Hermitage and Chapel of St. Katherine.

Such was the external appearance of London in the time when Richard Whittington came up from Pauntley, in Gloucestershire, to seek his fortune; great and glorious with its spires and towers, its stately houses, its broad river, noble bridge, its forest of masts, its crosses and conduits; squalid in its dirt and crowded houses; most glorious in the sturdy spirit of its people, in the freedom they had won, in their enterprise and patriotism, in their loyalty to the King who respected his charters, in their readiness to leave him and set up another king, as in the case of Richard the Second, when they conceived that their liberties were in danger. Freedom, they rightly thought, is a better thing than liberty; and it is wiser to guard the liberties of the State than to keep allegiance to a king.

[1] It was rebuilt, and made into the Hospital of St. John the Baptist, by Henry VII.

CHAPTER III.

THE COMPANIES AND TRADE OF LONDON.

"Advance the Virgin, lead the van;
  Of all that are in London free,
The MERCER is the foremost man,
  That founded a society.
Of all the trades that London grace,
We are the first in time and place."

IT was, then, into such a city that, in or about the
year 1371, young Whittington came to be apprenticed. His master was Sir John Fitz-Warren, a
Mercer and Merchant Adventurer. Fitz-Warren was
a younger son of that great House of Fitz-Warrens
who came to England with the Conqueror, and were
conspicuous in many ways, keeping themselves in the
foremost rank for many centuries, winning rich brides
at tournaments, getting lands in various counties and
losing them, defying kings, and leading the life of
Robin Hood in the forest, fighting valiantly, being
always found in the front, until, as seems to happen to
all families alike, there came the inevitable moment
when decadence set in, and the Fitz-Warrens should be,
for a time at least, quiet and forgotten. Sir John Fitz-

Warren was, like his prentice, a country lad, to begin
with. He came from North Devon, the same part of
the country as the Mansels, a daughter of whom was
Dame Whittington. He had connections also, like
the Mansels and the Berkeleys, in Somerset; in fact,
it is perfectly clear that he knew all about young
Whittington, and no doubt had already undertaken
to receive the boy, before he was sent up to London.
Would the widow of Sir William let her boy set
off for London unbefriended and helpless? West-
country folk, particularly those of good family, were
known to each other, and stood shoulder by shoulder
in those as well as in later days. Indeed, nothing
more certainly disproves the old "poor and friendless"
theory about young Dick Whittington than this fact,
that he was apprenticed to a Fitz-Warren. It is also
a remarkable proof of the position which London
traders held in those days, and the class which sought
to enter their ranks, to consider not only the birth of
Sir John Fitz-Warren, but also that of his wife Maud,
or Matilda, who was the daughter of one Agnes,
heiress of William de Peresford. She was three
times married—to John de Argentine, John de
Nutford, and Lord Maltravers. It is not known
which of the three was Maud's father. The family
history, however, of Fitz-Warrens and Whittingtons
alike, shows it was no unusual thing for the younger
sons of the best families to seek fortune in London

E

trade. We shall presently find an opportunity to speak of the life of a prentice of those days. We must now consider the position of the London Companies at the time when Whittington came to town, and especially of that famous and honourable Guild in which he was bound apprentice.

London was divided into Wards, nearly if not quite the same as now.[1] The richest, as appears from an assessment made in the year 1339, was that of Cordwayner Street. This was assessed at the sum of £2,195 3s. 4d. The next richest was Coleman Street, figuring at £1,051. The poorest was Aldgate, which was assessed at £30 only. The City was chiefly, though not entirely, inhabited by its craftsmen and tradesmen. As we have already seen, there were many great houses, such as Baynard's Castle, Cold Herbergh, and Tower Royal, which belonged to nobles and princes ; there were also monasteries and priories. Yet, on the whole, these great houses exercised little influence over the spirit of the place, which was entirely industrial and commercial. Princes and knights might come to the City and hold tournaments

---

[1] The Wards were as follows—Tower, Billingsgate Bridge, Dowgate, Langburn, Walbroke, Bishopsgate, Lyme Street, Cornhill, Cheap, Broad Street, Queenhithe, Cordwayner Street, Faringdon Street Within and Faringdon Street Without (they were separated in the reign of Richard II.), Cripplegate, Coleman Street, Candlewick Street, Aldgate, Portsoken, Castle Baynard, Bassishaw, and Aldersgate.

for the delight of the citizens ; kings might send messages that they wanted money ; but kings, princes, and knights never formed part of the life of the place, and from the earliest times the City officers have been City merchants.

London was perhaps as catholic in its commercial and industrial pursuits then as now. Every kind of trade was carried on within its walls, just as every kind of merchandise was sold. We are familiar with most of the fourteenth century crafts, but there are some which are now extinct or merged with others. For instance, we find the trades of " Plumier," " Fettermonger ;" " Wympler"—a wimple was the neck covering or kerchief used by women ; " Fannere," who made fans for winnowing corn ; " Pater-nostrer," or maker of prayer beads ; " Pinmaker ;" " Saucer," or dealer in salt ; " Tabourer," or maker of the little drums called tabours ; " Imageur," or maker of images for church purposes ; " Melemekere," probably a mallet maker ; " Selmakere," or seal maker ; " Knyf-smyth ;" " Kissere," probably a maker of armour for the thighs—*cuisses ;* " Selk-wyfe," a silk woman ; " Chaloner," or maker of "chalon," used for coverlets ; " Bureller," or maker of *burel,* a kind of coarse cloth ; " Disshere," or maker of dishes; "Pelterer," or skinner; " Wayte," or watchman ; " Walker," *i.e.,* a fuller who fulled at a walk-mill ; and many others.[1]

---

[1] Riley's " Memorials," p. xx.

The combination of fellows of the same craft began
in very early times. Long before the Norman Conquest the frith-guilds were formed for the protection
of the trade and its followers; the guild brothers met
once a-month to consider the interests of the craft;
and the London guilds in the time of Athelstan had
united together to form a merchant-guild for the purpose of controlling trade, gaining wider powers from
the Crown, regulating prices, recovering debts, and so
forth.

But this apparent freedom brought about a great
danger and a great tyranny. The governing body,
the Aldermen of the Wards, were taken from those
who had landed holdings in the City. But this was
a class which was comparatively small, while those
who had lost their original lot, or were escaped serfs,
had no share at all in the government of the City;
the merchant-guild had absorbed all the previously
existing guilds, and the new companies were only
beginning to be formed. Meantime, the discontent
caused by the assessments of the Aldermen, the
regulation of prices and hours, grew daily. Then the
unlanded craftsmen began to form themselves into
guilds, secretly at first, but presently, finding themselves unmolested, openly. Henry the Second, as
has been seen, fined these unauthorised companies,
and did the City the signal service of granting
Royal Charters to others; thus, one by one the com-

panies came into existence, the merchant-guild died out, and for a while London enjoyed a purely popular form of Government.

The time of Henry the Second was not, however, yet fully ripe for self-government. Among the companies formed then grew up jealousies and bickerings, trades overlapped each other, interests clashed, and men were as closely patriotic for their guilds as schoolboys for their schools. For instance, in the year 1226, there was a great quarrel between the goldsmiths and the tailors, whose interests, save in the matter of gold embroidery, could hardly be expected to clash. Yet they quarrelled, it matters not why, and presently turned out, to the number of 800 on both sides, armed with knives, sticks, clubs, and swords, and fought a battle royal in the streets. The grand principle of combination, however, once started, ran rapidly, and before many years all the tradesmen of London were banded together according to their mysteries, either in unauthorised guilds, or in companies holding letters patent of the King. Strange to say, the richest and most powerful company of all—the Mercers—was late in obtaining its letters patent. When Whittington was apprenticed, the company was yet but a guild.

It was a long time before the companies obtained, what they have ever since held, a monopoly of municipal offices and dignities. Little by little they parcelled out the inhabitants of London between them. They obtained from Edward the Second the law that no person should be admitted to the freedom of the City unless he were a member who had already served his full term of apprenticeship to a guild, trade, or mystery—that is, unless he were also admitted to membership in a City company. This freedom meant a great deal more than it means now. If a man is free in these days of the City, and therefore a member of a City company, he becomes eligible to the offices, dignities, and honours of the City; but in other respects he is no better off than those who are not free : in those days, without the freedom of the City he could not trade within the City walls; without the freedom of the City it was, therefore, impossible to live within the City. And the City suburb, which is now called Fleet Street, was also a part of Faringdon Street Without, under the jurisdiction of the City. Therefore, unless he held the freedom, a man must needs seek his living without the City. There was, to be sure, the Debateable Land, south of the Thames.

In the reign of Edward III. the fraternities began to adopt a distinctive dress : hence they were called the Livery Companies. The word "guild" gave place to "craft" or "mystery;" and the chief officer of the company, instead of being called the Alderman, a title now reserved for the head man of a ward, became the Master or Warden.

OLD HOUSES IN FLEET STREET.

Edward III. seems to have been the first king who realised the enormous importance of encouraging and fostering the trade of the City through its companies, and the necessity of furthering their development. Successful trade brought wealth to the country; wealth brought love of order—it also brought full bags for royal taxes ; love of order brought loyalty, sacrifices to the cause of order, devotion to the dynasty which represented order. Edward set the example—followed often enough since his day—of becoming a member of one of the companies, the Merchant Taylors, formerly called the Linen Armourers. Richard II., after his grandfather's example, became a member of the Mercers' Company. Princes and nobles followed the royal lead, and accepted membership of the great companies much as they do now.

In the same reign of Edward III., a great company was formed which threatened to swallow up and destroy all the rest ; it was the Company of Grossers, a fraternity of wholesale merchants who proposed to sell everything themselves instead of through the retail dealers. So great an opposition was offered to the enterprise, which anticipated certain great American "stores," that the King ordained that everybody should confine himself to one craft or mystery.

It may be interesting to enumerate the guilds and companies—some of which, including the Mercers, were not yet incorporated—existing in the year 1355, some fifteen years before Richard Whittington came to London.   They were as follows :—

Brasiers.	Bowyers.	Brewers.
Sporiers.	Ironmongers.	Salters.
Tanners (without Newgate.	Chandlers.	Cutlers.
	Pewterers.	Fishmongers.
Butchers (of St. Nicholas).	Tailors.	Mercers.
	Wax Chandlers.	Girdlers.
Butchers (of the Stocks).	Tanners without Cripplegate.	Prossers in the Ropery.
Grossers.	Pouchmakers.	Glovers.
Poulterers.	Cappers.	Armourers.
Curriers.	Vintners.	Goldsmiths.
Butchers of West Chepe.	Skinners.	Drapers.
	Leather-dressers.	

As regards their relative position and wealth, an assessment made at this time shows that the Mercers, Drapers, and Fishmongers were the richest of the companies, being rated at £41, £40, and £40 respectively.   The Brasiers were only called upon for £3 13s. 4d.; the Sporiers for 40s.; the Tanners, Poulterers, Pouchmakers, and Curriers for £1 16s. 8d. each; the Glovers for 20s.; and the Cappers for 13s. 4d.   The small and poor companies represented the mechanical trades, into which the sons of the poor freemen of the City were bound apprentice; while the more wealthy lads, and those of good family, attracted to London by its chances of fortune,

like young Whittington, went into the great companies. For there was then as great a difference as
there is now between a handicraftsman—one who
made spurs, buckles, pouches, blades, and sold them
at a stall—and one who made great bids for fortune,
had ventures on the seas, correspondence not only
with Bruges and Ghent, but also with Venice, Genoa,
and even Constantinople, owned a fleet which he
could, and often did, place at the disposal of the
King, and entertained as sumptuously as the King
himself. It was in the hopes of becoming such a
merchant that Richard Whittington came to town ;
not to be a working man sitting at a bench, or a
huckster bawling "come buy" at a stall spread with
ribbons. Could the son of Sir William, and the
brother of Sir Robert, High Sheriff of his county,
hope for less than to become the equal of Sir John
Fitz-Warren ?

It is noticeable that, towards the end of Edward
III.'s reign, the great companies began to separate
themselves from the smaller ones. The Mayor was
for some centuries elected exclusively from the rich
liveries. Even at the present day, a Lord Mayor,
unless he belong to one of the twelve great companies,
labours under certain disadvantages. He cannot, for
instance, become President of the Irish Society.

The general management of all the companies was
very much the same. The differences, indeed, were

those of different patron saints, different liveries, and different incomes. The first rule was that no base-born person or churl should be admitted to apprenticeship ; that no person should disclose the lawful secrets of the craft ; that no one should receive the freedom of the City until he had served his full term as an apprentice ; that apprentices should pay 3s. 4d. on entrance, and 5s. at least on receiving their freedom ; that masters should pay 20s. on taking an apprentice ; that no master was to employ a workman who had not served his time, and so on. The wardens had great powers, which they appear to have exercised zealously. They could visit everything, inspect everything ; especially they were to enquire into the quality of things sold, the honesty of the weights and measures—for instance, they kept a silver yard for the measure of cloths ; and because their duties, if carried out fearlessly, were apt to engender bad feelings among those of the craft who would cheat if they could, it was enjoined that every member of the company, if elected to the office of warden, was bound to serve ; and, further, that any member of the company not obeying the warden was liable to imprisonment. Thus when, in the year 1431, the Company of Brewers resolved that every man among them should send a barrel of ale for the solace of the King's army in France, and one Will Payne atte Swan, in Threadneedle Street (whether because

he was a Radical, and disapproved of the war, or out
of mere meanness), did absolutely refuse to contribute
his barrel, despising the orders of his wardens, and
using contumacious language, it was decided that he
be fined the sum of three shillings and fourpence,
which should be expended in the purchase of a swan
for the Master's breakfast. The obstinate Payne,
refusing this simple and good-humoured fine, and
therewith his share of the swan—for he would have
been invited to the breakfast—was forthwith haled to
prison. Strange to relate, he remained obdurate,
renounced the livery of his company, and defied
the authorities. He was therefore brought before
the Mayor, and at length, but after some time, it was
brought home to his understanding that, unless he
obeyed, imprisonment in a close and disagreeable
gaol from which fever was seldom absent would
inevitably follow, and further, that if, by some lucky
chance and the special blessing of Heaven, he should
survive Newgate, he would receive sentence of expulsion from the City, and consequent starvation would
be his lot. He then submitted. A very stubborn
and wrong-headed fellow! But no doubt from him
descended many a stiff-necked Roundhead and
modern Radical.

Another duty of the wardens was to assist the
poorer brethren, the decayed and infirm, the widows
and orphans of the livery. If a woman was married

to a freeman of the company, she became henceforth their daughter—they could not suffer her or her children to want.

The wardens also had to look that, by covetousness and overreaching, no member of their craft was injured by a brother of the same fraternity. They therefore forbade any to take a house or shop from a brother by offering a higher rent ; they forbade any to undersell each other ; they not only took care that there should be no cheating by under-weight or under-measure, but they fixed the prices, and they inflicted heavy penalties if the standard of good work was lowered. The hours of work were also fixed ; they were to be from daybreak until curfew.

In one of the companies—the Merchant Taylors, formerly called the Linen Armourers—their chief had another and more dangerous duty to perform. He travelled for the livery—probably to Flanders, to France, or to various parts of England, where broad-cloth was made. He was therefore called their " Pilgrim."

The courts of the companies were held four times a-year. They were summoned by a " Bedel," whose principal duty it was to call together the " Felliship." For this he received his livery, and, in the fourteenth century, the sum of fourpence a-week, which seems a small remuneration. Perhaps, however, something in the nature of board, some perquisite of beef, bread, and ale, some daily refection, was thrown in, for City companies have never been niggardly towards their servants. One feels quite sure that the "Bedel" was fat, lusty, well-fed, and contented. There were also in the service of every company a priest or chaplain ; a clerk, whose important duty it was to be the depository of the company's secrets, to guard the common seal, to keep the muniment room, and to enter the minutes of the meetings ; a cook—London cooks were ever famous caterers of toothsome dishes —with, one supposes and hopes, a competent and zealous staff of assistants ; there were, lastly, the warden's assistants, who were the clerks and account- ants, and kept the books.

The liveries were changed from time to time. Thus, that of the Grocers in the year 1414 was scarlet and green ; in 1418 it had become scarlet and black ; in 1423 it was "murrey and plunket"—that is to say, dark-red and blue.

The great day of the year was the company's saint's day. On this day all the members of the livery, great and small—from master and wardens to serving-men—kept high holiday, assembling in their hall, every man in a new livery, in the morning. First they marched to church in procession, headed by clerks, priests, and boys, all in surplices, singing as they went ; then came, each in his place, the sheriff's servants, the clerks, assistants, the chaplain, the Mayor's sergeants, often the Mayor himself, and, lastly, the Court, with prince or master, wardens, and officers.

After mass, they returned, in like order, to their hall, where dinner was laid for them ; the music was playing on the gallery ; the banners were displayed on the walls ; and the air was heavy with the scent of that precious Indian wood called sanders, which was imported to be burned on these occasions. Every sense was gratified at once. On the Hautpas, at the end of the hall, was the high table, where the Prime Warden, Master, or "Pilgrim" entertained the Court and the noble guests of the day ; below sat the Freemen, each (a practice fallen, unhappily, into disuse) accompanied by his wife, so that all alike might rejoice. And if no wife came—for the reason that his wife was sick, or that he might be a widower, or that he might be as yet unmarried—every member was invited and encouraged to bring with him a maiden— "*ameyne avec luy une demoiselle si luy plaist.*" No greedy feasting of the men among themselves, but the society of fair ladies, all in happiness together in courtesy and honour. Heard one ever more admirable provision for the joy of a fraternity ? Dinner over, the music in the gallery ceased for a while, and serious business was transacted—nothing less than the election of officers for the ensuing year. That happily despatched, the loving cup went round to refresh and cheer. History says nothing about how often the cup was filled, and how many times it passed round the hall; there are, however, two texts in the kitchen of the Fishmongers' Hall which we believe to have regulated every City banquet from time immemorial. They are golden texts. One enjoins the cooks to "WASTE NOT;" the other adds—lest these words should lead to parsimony—"SPARE NOT." Let us believe that the fourteenth century loving cup was replenished out of barrels, and that it went round and round, until the stoutest toper had had enough, and weak heads had long before desisted.

With hearts uplifted, then, with cheerful faces, and eyes aglow with pride in their own splendour, the honest craftsmen sat, every man with his wife or maiden beside him, while the minstrels led in the players, and interludes, allegories, and mummeries finished the great day of the year. The Freemen paid three shillings and sixpence each for their entertainment (this seems an enormous sum compared with the Bedel's weekly fourpence), and those who did not come paid two shillings and sixpence.

It is never disagreeable to read about feasting, and it is pleasant to know how our ancestors dined; therefore, the following bill of fare of a banquet of the fourteenth century will, I am sure, be read with interest. The mixture of sweets and meat in each course is contrary to modern ideas, and it will be seen that there is only one vegetable spoken of.

First Course.—Brawn, with mustard; cabbages in pottage; swan standard; cony, roasted; great custards.

Second Course.—Venison, in broth, with white mottrews; cony standard; partridges, with cocks, roasted; leche lombard; doucettes, with little parneux.

Third Course.—Pears in syrop; great birds with little ones together; fritters; payn puff, with a cold bake-meat.

With a little explanation, it will be perceived that here was a truly excellent dinner. One hopes, but with perfect confidence, that the wine was equal to the meats.

The *leche lombard* is said by one authority to have been a jelly of cream, isinglass, sugar, almonds, and other ingredients. Another authority states that it was made of pork pounded in a mortar with eggs, raisins, dates, sugar, salt, pepper, spices, milk of almonds, and red wine, all stuffed into a bladder and boiled.

Mottrews was a stew of pork and poultry pounded in a mortar and strained; afterwards it was "treated" with blanched almonds, milk, and the white flour of rice.

Doucettes were little sweetmeats and confections. *Parneux* were rich preparations of bread, &c. *Payn puffs* were made of bread stuffed with all kinds of *farces*—for example, marrow, yolk of eggs, dates, raisins, &c.

The citizens ate food long since discarded as coarse, such as lampreys and porpoise; they were fond of swans and peacocks; they used melted fat, or lard, for butter; for sugar they had honey; and they were especially addicted to eating furmenty, *i.e.,* wheat boiled in milk.

The Mercers' Company, which, until a great misfortune fell upon it early in the eighteenth century, was the richest of all the Liveries, was not incorporated until the year 1393, when they obtained letters patent of Richard II., with license to purchase in mortmain an estate of twenty pounds *per annum.* But there was a Guild of Mercers as early as 1172, and one of them, Robert Searle, was Mayor in 1214. At the end of the thirteenth century, a company of "Merchant Adventurers" sprang from the Guild of Mercers. The trade of the mercers at first was in "merceries," that is, in all kinds of wares, such as woollen cloths, ribbons, laces, and small finery; but by the time of Whittington the company contained a mixture of merchants—the said "Adventurers"—and of shopkeepers; and while the latter continued to keep their stalls on the south side of Chepe, between Bow Church and Friday Street, over against the Cross of Chepe, the former imported and sold wholesale or to great personages silks, satins, cloth of gold,

F

velvet, embroideries of precious stones, the fine stuffs from Belgium, Venice, and Genoa, and all the splendid materials required for the dresses of this most splendid period. In the time of Queen Elizabeth, their business lay chiefly in silk ; and Stow says that "these mercers are generally merchants." It was this company of merchants that Whittington joined, and it was to one of the richest and most eminent among them that he was apprenticed—another fact to disprove the "poor and friendless" theory.

As regards the livery of the company, it was repeatedly changed, and one does not know what it was in Whittington's time, but it was different from that of other companies in having the gown faced with satin instead of with budge, as was the general rule. They had also, in later times, a Pageant or Lord Mayor's Day, far more splendid than that of any other company. The Pageant met the Lord Mayor's procession on its return from Westminster. It was headed by a rock of coral with sea weeds, and Neptune mounted on a dolphin, with a throne of mother-of-pearl, and a company of tritons, mermaids, and so forth. Then came the famous "Maiden Chariot," grandiloquently described in 1686.

"An imperial triumphal chariot of Roman form, elegantly adorned with variety of paintings, commixed with richest metals, beautified and embellished with several embellishments of gold and silver, illustrated with divers inestimable and various coloured jewels of dazzling splendour, adorned and replenished with several lively figures, bearing the banners of the Kings, the Lord Mayors, and Companies, with the arms of the memorable King Richard the Second, the first and principal founder of this most ancient society. On a lofty ascent of which, exalted upon an imperial throne, sits a majestic person in great state, representing a Virgin, which is the arms of the right worshipful the Company of Mercers,[1] hieroglyfically attired in a robe or vestment of white satin, richly adorned with precious stones, fringed and embroidered with gold, signifying the graceful blushes of virginity ; on her head a long dishevelled hair of flaxen colour, decked with pearles and precious gems, on which is a coronet of gold beset with emeralds, diamonds, sapphires, and other precious jewels of inestimable value. Her buskins gold, laced with scarlet ribbons, adorned with pearles and other costly jewels. In one hand she holdeth a sceptre ; in the other a shield, with the arms of the right honourable the Company of Mercers."

Above the chariot was a canopy, on which Fame blew her trumpet, while Vigilance, Wisdom, Chastity, Prudence, Justice, Fortitude, Temperance, Faith, Hope, Charity, Loyalty, and the Nine Muses attended on the Maiden. Eight pages of honour walked on foot beside the chariot ; the charioteer was " Triumph;" the steeds were nine white Flanders horses, three abreast, each horse mounted by a person representing

---

[1] "Gules, a demy-virgin, with her hair dishevelled, crowned, issuing out and within an orb of clouds, all proper."—See the Cheapside entrance of Mercers' Hall.

something—on the first three, Victory, Fame, and
Loyalty ; on the next three, Peace and Plenty, with
Europe between ; on the the third three, Africa, Asia,
and America.   There were eight grooms and forty
" Roman lictors ;" twenty servants cleared the way—
they were themselves preceded by twenty savages, or
"green men," who threw squibs to keep off the crowd—
and the whole was followed by workmen, wheel-
wrights, and carpenters, ready to repair anything
which might get out of order in this great machine.
At the banquet which followed, the Maiden had a
separate table to herself and her attendant ladies.

The site of the present Mercers' Hall is that of the
ancient Hospital of St. Thomas de Acon—that is, St.
Thomas a Becket—called de Acon (Acre) in accordance with the legend of his mother's birth-place.
The hospital was built, twenty years after the Archbishop's murder, by Agnes, his sister, on the spot
where her brother was born.   Gilbert a Becket, the
father of the Archbishop, was himself a Mercer and
Portreeve of London.   The Church of St. Thomas
was on every Lord Mayor's Day attended in state
by the new Mayor and the Aldermen.   The Hospital
was sold to the Mercers by Henry VIII., and was
burned down in the Great Fire.

Whittington was master of his company in the
years 1398, 1407, and 1420, as many times as he held
the chief office of the City.   Among other distin-

guished masters and wardens of the company may be mentioned Sir John Coventry, one of Whittington's executors, and ancestor of the Earls of Coventry; Sir Geoffrey Bullen, or Boleyn, great-grandfather of Anne Boleyn; Sir William Hollis, from whom descended the Earls of Clare; Sir Michael Dormer, ancestor of the Earls Dormer; Sir Thomas Baldry, whose daughter married Lord Roch, ancestor of the Lords Kensington; Sir Thomas Seymour, from whom descend the Dukes of Somerset; Sir Baptist Hicks, ancestor of the Viscounts Camden, now extinct; Sir Rowland Hill, of the Lords Hill; James Butler, of the Earls of Ormond; Sir Geoffrey Fielding, of the family of the Earls of Denbigh; Sir Henry Colet, father of Dean Colet; and the greatest of all, next to Whittington, Sir Richard Gresham.

CHAPTER IV.

THE PRENTICE BOY.

"Gaillard he was, as goldfinch in the shaw."

WHEN, therefore, the boy entered London, he was provided with letters to Fitz-Warren, the great mercer, also a west-country man, who knew of what stock he came, and would receive such worldly goods as he had brought with him—a slender store, no doubt, but still something; a Whittington of Pauntley would not be sent to seek his fortune like a pauper.

Once apprenticed, and having in a few weeks imbibed the spirit of the place, the lad became a Londoner. It is one of the characteristics of London that he who comes up to the City from the country speedily becomes penetrated with the magic of the golden pavement, and falls in love with the great City. And he who has once felt that love of London can never again be happy beyond the sound of Bow Bells, which can now be heard for twenty miles round and more. The greatness of the City, its history, its churchyards crowded with dead citizens, its associations, its ambitions, its pride, its hurrying crowds—all these things affect the imagination and fill the heart. There is no place in all the world, and never has been, which so stirs the heart of her children with love and pride as the City of London ; not Paris even, nor Rome, nor Florence, nor Venice ; there is no city in which the people have been more steadfastly purposed to maintain their rights and fight for their freedom. "Presumptuous" sons of London, Froissart calls them.

Now it is remarkable that the history of London worthies is largely composed of the history of country boys who, like Whittington, have come to town to seek their fortune. The reason is not far to seek. The children of successful men are rarely as energetic as their fathers; they lack the stimulus; they are content to enjoy ; they need not work. Then the air of London, which stimulates and braces the country lad, seems to take the strength out of those who are born in it. So that one great citizen is rarely succeeded by another. The case of the Greshams only "proves" the rule. When the country lad comes to town, his brain is charged with vague ambitions, his eyes are filled with colour which makes everything that they see of a rosy hue. Nothing is so splendid as the Lord Mayor's Riding, nothing so much to be desired as the glory of the City ; were it only as a stimulus to the imagination of youth, the great city shows should be made as splendid as wit of man and wealth of corporation can devise. But how much more splendid were they in the fourteenth century than now! For black broadcloth, cloth of gold ; for black silk hat, a fur cap embroidered with gold and pearls ; fur-lined cloaks of scarlet, blue, and gold ; chains of gold ; gallant horses harnessed with gold embroidery ; troops of livery men in the colours of their companies ; silken banners worked with arms, which, to the eyes of those who looked on them, were as legible as printed book is now ; and, on occasions of simple every-day life, the Mayor, the Sheriffs, and the Aldermen going about with their sergeants, clad in robes of office, magistrates and judges to the open eye, with power to strike off the hand of him who dared resist their authority. Again, the merchants of the old time lived among their prentices and workmen ; their great state and splendour were things to be witnessed and envied of all. The clerk, now-a-days, cannot understand the glory of success, because he creeps home nightly to his suburban cottage at Camberwell, and never sees his master's gorgeous palace at Kensington, his galleries of pictures, his crowded balls, his sumptuous dinners. Formerly these things were done in the open, for all eyes to see ; and when the master entertained great lords, his prentices were there to see. As he was, so might they be.

Young Dick Whittington, then, was bound prentice to the Honourable Company of the Mercers, his
master being Sir John Fitz-Warren. He took, in some
fear and trembling, the vows of Industry, Obedience,
and Duty—vows far more useful than any designed
for the coward refuge of the Cloister; he entered
himself a soldier in the noble army of those who
have won the free right of work; and he promised—
though as yet he hardly knew the true meaning of
his promise—to carry on the structure of City rights,
until it should become the great Cathedral Church of
Liberty, which we call the Constitution of the Realm
of England.

It was in the early years of his apprenticeship that
he heard that famous carol of Bow Bells which so
warmed his heart. For my own part, I see no reason
to doubt it at all. I believe in the story, which, however, I read in my own way. Why, for instance, should
we believe in a poor boy sitting in sadness and dejection
upon the slopes of Highgate Hill? Why should the
boy be in sadness? He was a strong, active country
lad; his master was of his own country, and knew
his people; he must have been a just and kind man,
otherwise Whittington would not afterwards have
become his son-in-law; London life was joyous;
hope was in the air; the houses of rich men who had
made their own way were around him in every one
of the narrow streets. Why, instead of despair and

misery, I see a Dick Whittington standing with head
erect, bright eyes, and lithe limbs, alert, high-spirited,
brave, ready for any fortune, and sure in his own
mind of the best ; ambitious, too, and self-reliant.
What has lusty youth to do with tears ?   Below him,
four miles away, he sees the grey walls of London
town ; beyond the walls, a forest of spires : in every
church are the bones of those who died rich after
fighting the battle of freedom ; their souls are with
the just, because they have been good men, and have
left money for masses, to make all safe.   Within the
walls are countless treasures of merchandise ; within
them, too, the most noble and most free of all cities
in the world.   The thoughts of that great and noble
City, and the consciousness of belonging to it, fill his
heart with pride.   Beyond the city there is another
forest, the forest of masts.   Hundreds of English
vessels are there, loading and unloading ; they
belong to his master and his master's friends, the
Mercers and the Adventurers.   There is no part of
the great world, he thinks, whither the brave hearts
on board those ships will not venture—yea, even to
Constantinople, though the tents of the savage Turk
are already thick upon the Southern shores.   Then,
while he is in this mood, his head full of high
thoughts, there comes a message to the boy.   It
comes with the dash and clang of Bow Bells, and
cries aloud, " Whittington, Whittington, Whittington,

Lord Mayor of London!" Ring again, bells, mel-
lowed by the distance, and charged with words so
sweet! Turn again, boy; go home to work, that
message ringing in thy brain, in patience and in trust.

If Whittington was born about the year 1358, he
would be sent to London in his thirteenth or fourteenth year—that is, about 1371 or 1372. We may
remark, as a noteworthy fact, that at his very
entrance upon London life he would find the
citizens glorious with the recollection of a recent great
and patriotic achievement. It was in the year 1360
that the City of London, indignant at the depredations committed by French pirates on the coast
of Sussex, fitted out a fleet of 160 sail, with 14,000
men, to descend upon the coast of France; so that
no more, for some time, was heard of French pirates.
Or—but boys are not easily saddened by such things
—there was the memory of the great plague of 1362,
which carried off so many of the citizens. And in the
same year—to show that men should not live in constant terror of death—there had been the tournament
in Smithfield, in which many noble knights ran tilt,
and many foolish prentice boys lamented that they
could never make such brave show of skill with
lance and dexterity of horsemanship. Then, in
1363, there had been the most splendid of all
" Ridings," when the great merchant, Henry Picard
(late Mayor), entertained the Kings of England,

Scotland, France, and Cyprus, with the Prince of
Wales and a crowd of nobles—a greater day for
the City than that of the entertainment of the Allied
Sovereigns, for the Mayor of the fourteenth century
did what he of the nineteenth did not do—he sat at
the head of his own table.

A year or two later, the boy would learn, with his
fellow-prentices, that their sports and amusements
had fallen under the King's displeasure, and that they
must betake themselves to the neglected practice of bow
and arrow, "pellet and bolt," with a view to what
might happen. Moorfields was convenient for the
volunteers of the time. There was, however, never
any lack of excitement and novelty in the City of
London. Saw one ever a stranger company than
that band of a hundred and twenty Dutchmen, who
came over in the year 1368 to convert merry London
to sadness, and showed the loveliness of religion
practically by marching bare-backed, flogging each
other as they went, and chanting Psalms through the
streets of the City? Why they came, how they
fared, how long they stayed, does not appear; but
it is certain that their coming touched the religious
life of the people not one whit. Then, in the year
1369, the plague reappeared to scare the folk, and in
the autumn came a dearth of corn to threaten
them with starvation. In 1370 the Monastery of
the Chartreux was founded, upon the place which Sir

Walter Manny bought in 1349 for the poor creatures who died of the pestilence in that year of rebuke. And in 1372 there was the great jealousy of the City against foreigners, and it was hinted to Royalty that, unless civic rights were respected, there would be no more money for the fitting-out of fleets and the manning of ships for defence of the realm.

As for the manner of life which was led by the English, and especially the people of London, in those days, it may be found fully set forth in the pages of Chaucer, Piers Plowman, John Carpenter, Lydgate, and those "Memorials" of the City which have been collected and translated by Mr. Riley. In this chapter I propose to put together some of the ancient customs, and to show the kind of folk among whom the young country lad was to spend his days.

First of all, London was a city whose leaders, above all things, desired to maintain law and order; next, it was a city whose people were conservative of old customs. Thus, Fitz-Stephen, writing in the year 1174, says :—

" I think there is no city that hath more approved customs, either in frequenting the churches, honouring God's ordinances, observing holidays, giving alms, entertaining strangers, fulfilling contracts, solemnising marriages, setting out feasts and welcoming the guests, celebrating funerals, or burying the dead."

I do not know what connection, if any, a great merchant like Sir John Fitz-Warren would have with his humbler brethren of the same company, the Mercers, who had their stalls on the west side of Bow Church. One can hardly believe that he, too, would have a stall, with his apprentices to bawl, " What d' ye lack ?" and one cannot but suppose that then, as now, a great business such as Fitz-Warren's would require a considerable number of servants to keep the accounts and do the clerks' work. However, the Mercers' quarter was an admirably central place for witnessing the pageants and displays. We have no reason to doubt that in the matter of amusement and sight-seeing Whittington was like his fellows.

> " When ther any ridings were in Chepe,
>   Out of the shoppe thider would he lepe ;
>   And till that he had all the sight ysein,
>   And danced well, he would not come again."

There was plenty of liberty for the prentices, always a troublesome class to rule ; and though the hours of work for all trades were long—the blacksmiths, for instance, passed a law that work should not begin before six in the morning, nor go on after nine at night, except in the winter, when all should cease at eight—yet they had many holidays ; and the City was strict in its observance of the Sunday. This may be illustrated by a letter of the Archbishop of Canterbury to the Mayor and Aldermen, in which he complains that barbers work on Sunday, and urges them to take order thereupon :—" Seeing that the malice of man "—ecclesiastical language was then, as it is now, beautifully mild and gentle—" has so greatly increased in these days—a thing to be deplored—that temporal punishment is held more in dread than clerical, and that which touches the body or the purse more than that which kills the soul, we do heartily entreat you, and for the love of God require and exhort you, that, taking counsel therein, you will enact and ordain a competent penalty in money, to be levied for the chamber of your city, upon the barbers within the liberty of your city aforesaid." The fine enacted was six shillings and eightpence—a very great sum in these days. No doubt the barbers thereafter shaved no one but their friends on Sundays, and those only who came in by the back door—" such is the malice of man."

Prentices in every generation are more concerned with the recreations attainable than with the laws and administration of their trade. London citizens, old and young, delighted in games, shows, sports, and amusements. There were plenty for every season, so that one wonders how they found time for all. But, as we have said, there were many holidays, and Sunday was not a day of gloom. The calendar of sport begins with the New Year.

> "In January men do play
> In cards and dice their time away:
> Now men and maids do merry make
> At stool ball and at barley break."

January, indeed, was full of opportunities for revelry. The New Year brought gifts and good cheer.

> "These giftes the husband gives his wife and father eke
>   the child,
> And master on his men bestows the like with favour milde:
> And good beginning of the year they wish and wish again,
> According to the ancient guise of heathen people vaine:
> These eight days no man doth require his dettes of any man,
> Their tables do they furnish out with all the meat they can."

Twelfth Day, St. Agnes's Eve—when girls practised little divinations to find who would be their husbands— St. Paul's Day (Jan. 25)—

> "If St. Paul's Day be fair and clear,
> It does betide a happy year"—

all fell in this month, and brought amusements and feasting with them.

In time of frost the lads could skate and slide over Moorfields, whose swampy flat was covered here and there with shallow pools, which froze rapidly; in cold weather they could play at quarter-staff, at "hocking," at single-stick, at football, at bucklers. Every Friday in Lent there was horse riding and racing outside the walls; the custom of choosing a

valentine on the 14th February was not forgotten
Says John Lydgate—

> "Seynte Valentyn, of custom yeere by yeere
>   Men have an usaunce in this regioun
> To loke and serche Cupid's Kalendere,
>   And chose theyr choyse by grete affeccioun;
>   Such as ben prike with Cupid's nocioun,
> Taking theyr choyse as theyre sort doth falle;
> But I love oon which excellith alle."

On Shrove Tuesday there was cock-fighting in the
morning and football in the fields in the afternoon.
In the week before Easter a singular custom was
observed; they brought into every great man's house
a twisted tree (it is conjectured that this was in some
way an emblem of authority, just as courts were held
in France *sous l'orme*). There were the cruel sports
of bear-baiting, bull-baiting, cock-fighting, and
throwing at cocks going on all the year, but principally in the spring. At Easter they had sports
upon the water, rowing full tilt against a shield hung
upon a pole. There were other rejoicings at that
time. On one of the three days before Ascension
Day, the parson of the parish, accompanied by
churchwardens and parishioners, were wont to beat
the bounds, followed by the boys. On the first of
May the girls were abroad before dawn of day, and out
beyond the walls, to wash their faces in the dew;
but the prentices had been up all night cutting down

G

branches and adorning the Maypole with flowers, foliage, ribbons, and streamers. The houses were hung with flowers, wreaths, and tapestry. The Maypole was dragged to its place by oxen who wore flowers on their horns. When it was put up in its place, they erected summer houses, arbours, and bowers beside it. The Lady of the May presided over the dancing, feasting, and merriment, and for the day Cornhill looked as if it stood within the forest. There was morris-dancing with Robin Hood, Friar Tuck, the Fool, and Tom the Piper; there were hobby horses and pageants, with devils, monsters, and mummers of all kinds. But these were not confined to May Day.

On Midsummer Eve, the Vigil of Saint John the Baptist, there were bonfires, and the door of every house was decorated with green birch, long fennel, white lilies, St. John's wort, and garlands of beautiful flowers, with glass lamps, in which oil burned all the night. More music in the streets and dancing on this festival. All through the summer there were athletics, such as racing, shooting, wrestling, and putting the stone; and on every fine night the girls came out and danced for garlands. Then came miracle plays. On Bartholomew's Day there was wrestling before the Mayor and Sheriffs. On Holy Rood Day (Sept. 14) the lads would go a-nutting in Epping and Hainault Forests, or in the woods of

Hornsey. At Martinmass (Nov. 11) the approach of winter was duly welcomed with a feast.

> "It is the day of Martilmass ;
> Cuppes of ale should freely passe :
> What though winter has begun
> To push down the summer sun ?
> To our fire we can betake,
> And sit beside the crackling brake,
> Never heeding winter's face
> On the day of Martilmass."

At last came Christmas, with its mummings, disguisings, dances, feasts, and singing of Noels. The Lord of Misrule reigned from All Hallows' Eve to Candlemas Day. At this season the houses and churches were decked with holm, ivy, bays, and all green things that could be procured ; and the last week of the year was passed in that mixture of religious rites, gay shows, dancing, pageants, and feasts which were so dear to London citizens of every degree.[1]

---

[1] The following, from a MS. of the 15th century, gives a list of the amusements throughout the year :—

" At Yule we wonten gambol dance to carol and to sing,
To have good spiced sewe and roast and plum-pie for a king ;
At Easter-eve pam-puffes ; Gangtide Gates did holy messes bring ;
At Pasque began our Morris, and ere Pentecost our May,
Though Robin Hood, lyle John, Friar Tuck, and Marian deftly play,
And Lord and Lady gang til kirk with lads and lasses gay :
Fra mass and e'ensong so good cheer and glee on every green,
As save our walles, 'twixt Eames and Sibbes, like game was neere seen.

We must not forget the processions, "chevauchés," and ridings continually taking place for some city function or some royal visit—the Mayor's Riding, the Procession of the Liveries, the Parade of the Cressets on the Eve of St. John the Baptist. On that night the whole of the City Watch, 2,000 strong, used to turn out in a great procession: 940 men carried cressets; each had an attendant. There were 2,000 of the Marching Watch. The Archers were clad in white fustian, with the arms of the City on back and breast; the Pikemen had bright corslets. There was the blare of trumpets and the beating of drums; there were great standards. The Mayor came after, mounted on horseback; his sword-bearer before him in fair armour, about him footmen and torch-bearer, and after him his watch, his giant, and his pageant. The Sheriffs followed with their pageants; and there were the morris dancers and mummers following after—a gallant show. Then there were the ecclesiastical grand days—the processions of monks, priests, and choristers, with the music in the churches, every city function being connected

---

At Baptist Day, with ale and cakes, 'mid bonfires neighbours stood;
At Martinmass we turned a crab, then told of Robin Hood,
Till after long time merk, when blest were windows, doors, and lights,
And pails were filled and hearths were swept 'gainst fairy elves and
    sprites;
Rock and Plough Monday games shall gang with Saint feasts and kirk
    sights."

with a church service and a procession ; whispers meanwhile in plenty, anent the private conduct of the priests, which in this fourteenth century had reached almost its worst. The great City holydays were Christmas Day, Twelfth Day, Easter Day, St. John the Baptist on June 24th, and St. Peter and Paul on June 29th. In order to prevent drunkenness on the last two days, which fell in the hot summer—we must not forget to render account of the old style, which puts everything eleven days in advance—and in those nights when there is no darkness but only a clear twilight, it was ordered that no vintner, brewer, taverner, cook, baker, or huckster was to sell anything after ten o'clock. Again, there were the occasions on which the City magistrates rode out to welcome the Court, or to receive illustrious visitors, or to a *Te Deum* at Paul's for a victory, or to follow in the train of a great funeral. And there was the Saint's Day of every City Company.

These were the regular and properly constituted amusements. We must add to them the excitements of the daily life—the bustle and stir, the movement and noise of the great City, the tumults among the turbulent citizens, the quarrels of the Companies, the fights and brawls in the streets, the uprisings against foreign residents, all of whom were regarded with jealousy and suspicion by London citizens as late as the last century. In the time of Whittington

they seem to have passed their days in continual terrors
and dangers. When, as happened in the rebellion of
Wat Tyler, a commotion became a rising, the Masters
and members of the Liveries gathered themselves
together for self-defence and the restoration of order.
Thus Froissart relates that in that great and
dangerous rebellion, while the rebels were burning
the Savoy, plundering the Tower, and destroying
the Priory of the Knights Hospitallers, the citizens
of London were quietly gathering together and
arming in their houses. Sir Robert Knolles, for
example, remained in his own house, with six score
companions, resolved to defend his property to the
last. And when the King rode forth to meet the
insurgents, on the spread of an alarm that his life was
in danger, 8,000 citizens instantly collected together,
all fully armed. Now this was a sight for a prentice
boy to remember.

There was another amusement greatly in favour
with all classes of the middle ages—going a pilgrimage. The monotony of life was relieved by these
delightful expeditions, in which every kind of
pleasure was found—change of scene, society, feasting, and even music, for no party was made up that
did not contain some who could sing or play.
The places most in favour in England were Canterbury, Beverley, Walsingham, and Glastonbury, where
they showed the Sacred Thorn. Sometimes, how-

ever, they went farther afield, and found across the
sea spots even more sacred, such as Toulouse or
Rome, or even Jerusalem—the Wife of Bath had been
three times to Jerusalem. Chaucer shows how a
party of pilgrims embraced all sorts and conditions of
men. As for the poorest, the villagers, they were not
allowed to go without letters patent, a kind of pass
granted by the Lord of the Manor and the parish
priest. For it was found, in France more than
in England, that the desire to go a pilgrimage grew
into a desire to leave wife, children, and work, and
tramp joyously, living at the monasteries, from place
to place. It was not, however, permitted to prentices
to indulge in this pious pastime.

One word more on the London amusements. The
City has always been famous for its taverns, clubs,
and coffee-houses. There were already, in the four-
teenth century, many famous places of resort, where
men could sit together, and drink and sing. The
principal of them were the *Salutation* of Billingsgate ;
the *Boar's Head* of London Stone ; the *Swan*, at
Dowgate, convenient for Prince Hal when he was at
Cold Herbergh ; the *Mitre* of Chepe ; the *Mermaid* on
Cornhill ; the *Three Tuns* of Newgate Market ; the
Windmill of the Exchange, and the *King's Head* of
New Fish Street.

We may readily imagine the joy, for a lad fresh
from the country, to live in such a city, to see such

pageants, to take part in the noisy, busy, and active life around him ; to feel, day by day, wonder changing into ambition, and astonishment into hope, as he began to understand it all. We may picture the boy wandering to the crowded banks of the Thames below bridge, rowing about among the shipping, clambering on board and talking to the sailors, feeding his imagination with the talk of the grizzled old captain, who

> " Knew well all the havens as they were,
>   From Gothland to the Cape de Finisterre,
>   And every creek in Bretagne and in Spain."

Why, what was the country life, even with its hunting and sport, its perils from robbers, and its fresh, sweet air, compared with this great and wonderful city, whose very pavement was of gold, whose magazines were crammed with things beyond all price, whose treasures were brought to its shores by ships that had braved cruel pirates, and infidels accursed, and many a tempest upon the cruel seas ?

So much for the amusements and joys of London. But there are other aspects of the City ; nor was it altogether for pastime that Dick Whittington was sent up to London. The City had its darker side. First, the hours of work were long, the discipline of prentices was severe, and the life hard ; authority made itself felt. Then there were the dangers of brawls continually arising, in the settlement of which knives were as freely used as, in the last century, clubs and fists. There were the dangers of the City from the extortions of kings, which were felt in all classes ; there were the dangers of fire, of civil war, of famine, and of pestilence. " From plague, pestilence, and famine" we pray, weekly, to be delivered ; but what meaning do we attach to the words, compared with those who could remember, or had heard of, a pestilence which killed two-thirds of London citizens, and famines when the people were fain to give their all for a morsel of bread ? As for the noisome smells, the bad ventilation, the filth of the City, I suppose they were no more felt by the peop.. than is the same thing in a town of Southern France —say Narbonne. Then there were the dangers from rogues. Where there is wealth there are rogues, who would fain be plundering. London has always been rich in rogues, thieves, and plotters against such as have property. It was, no doubt, a distraction in those days to witness the punishments which were inflicted in the open air, before the eyes of all, for a deterrent. No doubt, when the offender was known to all who looked on, the shame and suffering he underwent became an admonition to the bystanders. Thus there was the chopping off of the right hand of those who struck a sheriff or alderman, unless the offended officer himself asked that the offender should

be pardoned. There was the hanging of burglars ; but
burglary was rare, because the mind of the City was
well known on the subject of house-breaking, and no
mercy was to be expected for one caught in the
act. We must remember that every man kept his
own money in his own house—a fact which explains
clearly the strong feeling entertained on the sinfulness
of burglary.

Then it was exciting to witness the solemn march
down Chepe of a procession, consisting of the Mayor's
sergeants, escorting a man or woman dressed in a
white shirt, and bearing a wax taper of three pounds
weight, performing the *amende honorable.* Now and
then it was possible to witness a grand beheading on
Tower Hill, with subsequent quartering, for treason,
though these cases were rare. Sir Nicolas Brembre,
ex-Mayor, however, was thus beheaded in Whittington's time, and no doubt before his eyes--a
striking example of the mutability of fortune. A
spectacle to be witnessed every day, however, or
nearly every day, was the punishment by Pillory and
Thewe. As regards the latter, it was a machine
designed for the punishment of women. They sat in
a kind of chair like a ducking-stool, or stool of
repentance. Raised above the crowd, they had head
and feet uncovered, and were supposed to be sub-
jected to the derision of the crowd. The London
Thewe was set up on Cornhill, near the prison called

the Tun, which was taken away in the reign of
Richard II. to make room for a conduit.

As yet we are far from the brutal punishments
which came in later. Heretics are not yet burned;
ears are not sliced off, nor noses slit; there is no rack
in England; torture by boot, by water, by pulleys,
has not yet been invented; the cruel punishments
inflicted on criminals in France are not known in
England; there is no flogging of men and women
at the cart-tail, no whippings in bridewell, none of
wretched pickpockets in the presence of aldermen, no
branding of the hand. The Criminal Code of London
is unwritten; there is no scale of punishments; each
case is tried on its own merits, and a door seems
always open to favour if the delinquent repents and
promises. The reason of this mildness does not seem
far to seek; it is because, although the city must
have contained upwards of 200,000 inhabitants, the
aldermen, each in his own ward, knew everybody;
they were, consequently, not disposed to press a
delinquent too hardly. Admonition, timely rebuke,
was better than an open shame. Again, there was one
penalty always in reserve, far more severe than any
subsequently devised punishment, harder almost than
death—banishment from the City, and deprivation of
the privileges of a freeman. There was also, it is
quite certain from the conduct and bequests of Whittington and others, an ever-present feeling that prison

meant certain fever and probable death. For whatever causes, however, the fact is clearly established
by the civic records, that the Mayor and Aldermen,
in the reigns of Edward III., Richard II., Henry IV.,
and his son, placed unbounded confidence in the
pillory. Whatever was the offence—pillory. Where,
in the eighteenth century, death was certain, as in
shoplifting and forgery, in the fourteenth, pillory was
considered quite severe enough to meet the case.
Pillory was the universal reformer ; pillory was the
most dreaded punishment ; pillory was the sentence
passed upon all offenders alike ; pillory for one hour,
pillory for two, pillory for three. After pillory and
repentance, a full forgiveness was generally extended
to the criminal ; not always, however, as in the case
of William Frankyshe, who pretended to be son of the
Earl of Ormond, and so cheated John Tylneye, a
simple gentleman of Norfolk, out of much money.
He was not only set in the pillory for three hours,
but was also sent to Newgate, there to remain until
he should satisfy John Tylneye, and the Mayor
should see reason for his release.

The Ten Commandments may be broken in a great
variety of ways, but the charge-sheet at a Police Court
seldom shows any form of crime which is not perfectly familiar to the magistrates and officers. It is
interesting, however, to find that the Mayor's Court
in the reign of King Richard the Second heard

cases of much the same nature as the Mansion-House
Court of the present day, with this difference, that
the cases were treated summarily, and, most often,
were dismissed with the infliction of a punishment
which, to our modern offender, would seem indeed
ridiculous. When, for instance, Alan Birchore,
stringer by trade, was found to have sold four
dozen bow-strings, all " false and deceptive," it was
thought sufficient punishment to set this rogue in the
pillory for one hour, and to burn his fraudulent
strings before his eyes. Again, Thomas Stokes,
who pretended to be an officer and " taker of ale " of
the Royal Household, and, under that guise, went to
divers brewers and marked casks with the broad
arrow, receiving sums of money to let the said casks
remain, had an hour of pillory. The case of William
Northampton, cobbler, is even more remarkable, considering what a great deal of trouble he gave, and
that a single hour of pillory was considered full and
sufficient punishment. The case was this. Alice,
the wife of Andrew Trig, a woman of great respect-
ability, had the misfortune to lose a kerchief made of
fine Paris thread. The theft was imputed, whether
rightly or wrongly, to another Alice, wife of John
Bynthum. The charge was so grievous to the
accused, that, not knowing how else to clear herself,
she went to William Northampton, cobbler, and asked
his good offices, imparting to him secret information

about the said Alice, wife of Andrew Trig. Thereupon, the crafty cobbler repaired to Alice, and,
showing that by his skill he knew this and that
secret, pretended that he knew all others, and
especially the thief of the kerchief; that it was not
Alice, wife of John; and that, for her defamation
and spreading of false reports, she should be punished
by dying within a month. Upon this, the unfortunate
Alice fell into so profound a fear that she nearly died
before the end of the month, and would certainly
have fulfilled the cobbler's prophecy but for his
arrest, confession, and pillory, one result of which was
that she got better.

The soldier wounded in the wars is an old friend
in every age. There was, therefore, nothing original
in the deceit practised by Hugh de la Pole, a Welsh-
man, who bandaged his hand with a handkerchief
steeped in oil, and told how he was hurt at the siege
of Ypres, with many details, all of them fabrications,
about the conduct of that military operation. He,
too, received an hour of pillory.

The case of Robert Berewold is akin to that of the
cobbler. There was, one day, great stir in the house
of the Lady Matilda de Eye, of St. Mildred Poultry,
anent a certain "mazer" (a cup circled with silver or
silver gilt), which was lost. One Alan, a water-bearer
of the establishment, being exercised in mind on
account of the said cup, went to Robert Berewold,

and begged him by magic art to discover unto him
the thief. Thereupon, this impudent varlet took a
loaf of bread, and fixing in the top of it a round peg,
with four knives at the four sides of the same, in
form like a cross, pronounced certain words, and then
informed the inquirer at this oracle that Johanna
Wolsey had stolen the cup. Alan, a simple man,
believed, and defamed Johanna accordingly. The
result was that Robert had an hour of pillory, the
loaf, knives, and all being hung about his neck,
and that Alan was ordered to stand up in church
and confess that he had defamed Johanna. A similar
case was that of Nicholas Pot, a Dutchman, who, also
for a lost mazer, pretended by magic to name the
thief, and stood in pillory.

Another crime thus punished was that of a certain
Roger Cleek, of Wandelsworth—one would not have
suspected a native of that secluded village of such
guile—who pretended to be a physician. This im-
postor went to the house of John Atte Hatch, in
"Ismonger" Lane, where Johanna, wife of the aforesaid Hatch, lay ill in bed. He looked at the patient,
professed that he could cure her, and on the faith of
that profession John paid him twelvepence in advance
—a half of his fee. Roger thereupon tied a parchment round the neck of the sick woman, and went his
way, twelvepence in pocket. Contrary to reasonable
expectation, the remedy did the poor creature no

good at all. Charged with the offence of deceit,
Roger impudently declared that the parchment had
certain words written upon it which were sovereign
against fever. On opening the parchment, not a
word of any kind, good or bad, was found upon it.
The Court, after remarking with severity that a straw
in the shoe would have been quite as good for the
patient, ordered the quack to be set upon a horse
without a saddle, and then, preceded by pipe and
trumpet, to be ridden through the City, certain well-
known vessels of the medical art hung round his neck,
and, lastly, to be set in the pillory for one hour. No
doubt the prentices ran joyously to see the spectacle.

Let us illustrate the manners of the time by a few
more cases. John Roos, " Esquire," entered into a
conspiracy to defraud James de Pekham of £1,200 by
means of a false bond. One would think, considering
the vast sum at stake, that a signal punishment would
have been inflicted. The sentence was pillory for
one hour, the said false bond hanging from the neck
of the forger. This was in the year 1377. In 1777
he would have been hanged ; in 1877 he would have
been transported for life.

When Ralph atte Sele, baker, had been condemned
and fined for selling bread of short weight, he went
about reviling the Mayor, and declaring that his
loaves had been found of short weight because they
were not weighed when hot, whereas the present case

had been taken in weighing the loaves when they came from the oven. Such a case could not be overlooked, and Ralph stood in the pillory with a whetstone round his neck, to show to all that here was a convicted liar.

William Pykemyle got not only an hour of pillory, but was also turned out of the City for pretending, the impudent rogue, to be the bearer of a message from the King, and thereby getting forty pence from the Countess of Norfolk.

A notable brace of impostors were John Warde and Robert Lynham. These worthies paraded the streets, bearing each an ell measure. This was to show that they were traders. One carried a great red piece of leather, on which were written the words—" This is the Tongue of John Ward," and the other bore a terrible and suggestive iron hook with a pair of pincers. Both pretended to be dumb, and, opening their mouths, pointed to the absence of their tongues, and then to the hook and pincers, thus mutely leading the credulous to believe that they had been taken prisoners on the high seas or in foreign parts, and despitefully used by robbers or pirates. Money was freely contributed for the relief of these unfortunates, who, however, were haled before the Court, and found to have tongues, and as good as any. Therefore, pillory for three hours, and imprisonment till released by order.

H

Thus three sturdy rogues vanish out of sight. They are followed by poor old John Bernard. He was advanced in years; and one day, tempted of the Devil, he fell into sin, bringing up to London, on his four pack-horses, eight sacks of charcoal, each sack representing one quarter, but, alas! of light weight, being a bushel short. For this offence, he was sentenced to the pillory, and to have his sacks burned; but by reason of his age, the Court adjudged that he should remain no longer than for the burning of his sacks. So the old man drove his pack-horses home that night without his sacks, and was, we may suspect, a good deal upset by the excitement and the fear.

For selling putrid pigeons—pillory; for cheating with a chequer-board—pillory, with restitution of stolen money; for defrauding by false dice John Thomson and William de Glendale of Dumfries—two credulous Scotchmen—out of forty shillings, and a knife worth five shillings—pillory, with restitution; for saying falsely that the Mayor had been sent to the Tower—pillory; for pretending to be an officer of the Marshalsea, and going about with a tipstaff—pillory; for pretending to be a collector for Bethlehem Hospital—pillory; for making unsound barrels—pillory, with burning of the barrels before the prisoners; for stealing a baselard at a funeral —pillory; for selling bags filled with rape seed,

roots of radish, and *setuwall*, rotten and unfit
for use, for ginger, tansy seed for *wormseed*, rosin
for frankincense—pillory ; for pretending to be
the servant of a nobleman, and in that disguise
obtaining rich stuffs—pillory ; for forging title-deeds
—pillory ; for stealing a leg of mutton—pillory ; and
so on, through the pages of the civic records. Pillory
serves for all. As to the manner of punishment, it
probably differed little in the fourteenth century from
that of later times. There are many pictures extant
representing pillories, and criminals in them. In one
of these, shown by Douce, there is a large circular
ring about four feet high, in which are four women,
confined by the hands and neck. In another there is
a cage, with " accommodation " for six, elevated to a
height of apparently fifteen feet. In another a woman
is simply held by an iron collar to a post, standing on a
ledge some four feet from the ground. In a fourth, a
post is fixed in the ground, and has a hole in it,
through which the offender has to put his head.
Another, like the pillory of the last century, has a
cross-board for head and hands, and the criminal's
name " writ large " over his head.

It is impossible to judge of the severity of this
favourite punishment, or its deterrent effect. No
doubt it would be very great upon a freeman of the
City. When we consider the pride which every
citizen took in his Company and in his privileges, it

would be a very dreadful thing for a freeman, a
craftsman of a livery company, to be thus held up
to public contempt ; a common rogue, like John
Ward with his hook and pincers, would only dread it
so far as it would make his face known, and he could
practise his deceit no longer in London ; he would,
too, speedily find himself outside the City gates. Then
the question arises as to how far the shame of the
pillory was mingled with fear of dead cats, rotten
eggs, and such missiles, with which, in later years, a
pillory bird was regaled.   If the sentences of the
courts were lenient, manners were rough and
prentices pitiless.   Unfortunately, the civic records
are silent as to the behaviour of the mob and the
sufferings of the culprit.   One thing may be remarked—no man comes before the Mayor charged
with being an habitual criminal.   A thief might be
detected once, and put in the pillory ; but for a second
offence, outside the gates must he go.   The maintenance of law and authority was to be enforced by
rougher lessons than an hour of pillory.   Thus, when
Walter Constable, tailor, assaulted a ward constable,
he found himself imprisoned for forty days, and fined
no less a sum than a hundred shillings—a warning to
the citizens.   When John Arkwythe lost his head,
and took the Sheriff by the breast and shook him,
he was sentenced to imprisonment for a year and
a day, and to be discharged from the freedom of

the City. Thomas Maynelle, grocer, was charged
before the Mayor, by Alderman Sevenok, with certain
irregular and sinister doings and sayings, and divers
damages, dissensions, disputes, and losses. On being
reprimanded, he menacingly said to the same alderman that he had best look to himself, lest such an
end should befall him as befel Sir Nicolas Brembre,
ex-Mayor, who was beheaded. This contempt of
authority was met with a sentence of imprisonment for
a year and a day, and, after, to lose the freedom of the
City. Yet, when the prisoner humbled himself, the
good alderman entreated his pardon, which one is
glad to learn was granted him.

If authority and dignity of office might not be
brought into contempt, so it must not be refused, as
is shown by the case of John Gedeney, draper, who
thought he might refuse the office of alderman, and
did so, alleging insufficiency and inability. The
Court gently reminded him of his oath as a freeman,
by which he was made a partaker in Lot—that is, in
liability to take office; and in Scot—that is, in liability
to taxation. Yet the said Gedeney stubbornly refused. Thereupon, an example was made of him; he
was committed to prison, his shop was shut up, his
goods sequestrated. At these high-handed measures,
Gedeney saw that he must submit, and did so, being
at once forgiven and received into favour. Some
years later he became Mayor.

A less intelligible resistance to the law is that of
William Kyngscote, who was Warden of Ludgate.
When the newly-elected Sheriffs came to take over
the prisoners, as was their custom and their duty,
they were received by the said William with a flat
refusal to give up the prisoners, and on their endeavouring to force a way into the prison, they were met
with stones, swords, sticks, and baselards, so that
they were fain to retire, to the great scandal of all
right-minded citizens. But at the appearance of a
large force he submitted. He was sentenced to imprisonment for a year, deprivation of his office, and
never again to be allowed to hold any post in the
City. But on his supplication for pardon he was
released, and shortly afterwards he was reinstated,
the reason alleged for the said reinstatement pointing
to the probable cause of his rebellion, viz., that he
had laid out money upon the gate and the prison.
One imagines the honest but hot-headed Warden
expending all he could afford, with great zeal, for the
repair of the prison, and, bill sent in, not being able
to get it paid. But one must not, therefore, bring
out baselards to fight the Sheriffs.

A very curious crime, of which more than one
example is found in the records of this time, was the
forgery of Papal Bulls. One Lawrence Newport, by
means of forged Bulls, with a seal of lead, purporting
to be from " the Most Holy Father in Christ, and

Lord, the Lord John, twenty-second of that name,"
presented a Bill of Plurality to his brother, and provided himself with a " Corrody" — that is, a bill
authorising him to draw for a monthly allowance
of money, food, or clothing upon the Abbot of
Malmesbury. When this Lawrence appeared in the
pillory, his neck was ornamented with the forged
Bulls. Why, up to fifty years ago Lawrence would
have been hanged! In Queen Mary's time he would
probably have been burned.

William Blakeney, shuttle-maker, seems to have
been a man of ready wit and great ingenuity. He
went about the City with long hair, and barefoot, pretending to be a hermit ; and he would relate to all
comers moving stories and strange adventures
encountered on his pilgrimages, saying that he
had been even as far as Jerusalem, and kissed
the Holy Sepulchre, and to Rome, where he had seen
marvels, and to Venice, and to Seville. And by the
stories which he told—the English being always fond
of travellers' tales, and of hearing how men live *outre
mer*—he managed to get along in great comfort and
luxury, beyond the profession of a hermit or the
position of a shuttle-maker, for six long years. Then
fate came upon him, and he, too, after confession and
submission—because, no doubt, the case was quite
clear against him—was fain to place his head in that
shameful hole of pillory, a sight for all, a liar and

deceiver, and so perhaps back to shuttle-making, a poor trade, yet with his imagination still active within him, and many most beautiful stories suppressed and lost, or thrown away upon his unbelieving family.

Besides these trials, there were plenty of off-hand, rough-and-ready acts of summary justice, and laws which seem to interfere with the liberty of the subject. One Simon Figge, a Sandwich man, must needs spread reports of assaults and outrages in this peaceful city. To prison with him until further notice! No foreigner was allowed in the streets before six in the morning or after six in the evening; no citizen was to be in the streets after nine at night. As there were no police to watch the streets, but only occasional patrols, these laws must have been broken with impunity. No one was allowed to go armed unless of the rank of a knight; no one was to build over the street. The price of commodities was constantly being fixed. As regards the value of money, we find the guardian of a girl of respectable parentage charging her eightpence a-week for board and lodging, eightpence a-week for clothes, and eightpence a-week for doctoring, dressing her head, teaching her, providing her with shoes, and all other expenses; in other words, a young woman of the citizen class cost about two shillings a-week to keep respectably and to educate. But we find the son of a knight charged for his board and lodging and the maintenance of his servants—it is not said how many servants—five shillings a-week. The stalls for the butchers and bakers round the Cross of Chepe were let at an annual rent of thirteen shillings and fourpence each, those near Paul's Cross at ten shillings each. The prices of provisions may be gathered from the following list, which was fixed in the year 1374. By the end of the century they would be somewhat advanced.

	£	s	d
The best grass-fed ox alive, ...	0	16	0
The best grain-fed ox, ...	1	4	0
The best cow, ...	0	12	0
The best hog, of two years old, ...	0	3	4
The best shorn mutton, ...	0	1	4
The best goose, ...	0	0	3
The best capon, ...	0	0	2½
The best hen, ...	0	0	1½
The best chickens, two for	0	0	1½
The best young pigeons, three for ...	0	0	1
Twenty eggs, ...	0	0	1

It has been already hinted that there were often jealousies and dissensions between companies, or between master and men. In these cases the City was peremptory. When, for instance, the cobblers and the cordwainers quarrelled, it was ruled that no person who meddles with old shoes shall meddle

with new shoes, and every manner of work that may
be made of new leather belongs to the cordwainers.
So that was appeased. When, as now and then
happened, the journeymen tried to form themselves
into companies for the good of wages, the City
instantly put them down. No "covies" or combinations of journeymen were allowed on any
pretence. The saddlers, for example, instituted a
trades union of their own ; so did the cordwainers,
who formed a congregation, and defied the overseers.
The journeymen tailors banded together in companies,
living in houses of their own, and working for themselves, and had in the end to be turned out of the
houses they had occupied ; for all these combinations
and societies were sternly put down. Within the
Companies, the honour, dignity, and authority of
Master, Wardens, and Court had to be considered
before anything else. And if this was so at meetings
of the Liveries, with much more care was the dignity
of the civic authorities upheld. Thus a certain ill-
conditioned burgess, who had himself been raised
to the honour of an alderman, was heard to revile
the City laws openly and without restraint. On the
matter being brought before the Mayor, he was
punished by being forbidden to wear any vestment
belonging to or signifying civic distinction, such as a
cloak lined with silk or furred with budge. Moreover, he was expelled from whatever offices, great

or small, he was then holding, and reduced to the condition of a simple citizen. Another story illustrates the jealousy of the Corporation as regards its authority. It was agreed between the Mayor and Aldermen that on the day of Pentecost they should appear in new cloaks of green, lined with green taffetas. On the day appointed, Alderman John Sely appeared in a cloak without the lining. He was fined a dinner.

Three or four points are made abundantly clear from these memorials of old City life. The greatest respect was claimed for and paid to the City officers; their jurisdiction embraced everything, even the prices at which provisions were to be sold. They regarded an open and public exposure as the worst of punishments. For a hardened offender, expulsion from the City was the only penalty. In cases of insubordination, disrespect, or contempt of court, they were rigorous to outward seeming, yet there was ever a door opened for submission and pardon.

Another thing: the functions of the Mayor's Court were not limited; they extended over all kinds of cases. Sometimes the City even invaded rights ecclesiastical. Thus, because some of the parsons of the City churches refused to take their legal fee for baptism and the like—this was one farthing—the Mayor ordered that no poor person should pay more; nor should even rich men pay more than forty pence

for a baptism, or more than half-a-mark for a
wedding, unless it were that of a son, or daughter, or
some one near of kin. Laws were even passed
against idle babbling; and when the City was
agitated about certain disputes, it was enacted that
no one should venture to pronounce an opinion. A
certain beadle, too, having been found to have gone
about spreading false and gossipy reports, was
dismissed his office, with a promise of favour if he
could find the man who told him these things. One
sadly pictures the unfrocked beadle roaming up and
down the streets, heedless of the throng and bustle,
which interested him no more, anxious only to meet
once more the face of that stranger who so wickedly
misled him. As for that other case of John Constantyn, cordwainer, who was hanged, one feels scant
pity for him, because he went the length of shutting
up his shop, and inciting his fellow-citizens to do the
like. What greater disrespect to the Mayor of a city
of industry than to put up the shutters in broad day-
light? As for mere defamation and personal reviling
of special officers, the injured person generally begged
that the mercy of the Court should be extended to
the culprit, satisfied for himself with the vindication
of his honour.

There were customs, too, among the London
people which a lad from the country would have to
learn, as well as many customs and many tricks of

speech which he would have to unlearn. For instance, the village lad of Pauntley would be struck with some astonishment at the "glutton" masses which the people of this wonderful city held five times every year in honour of the Virgin. At these masses the worshippers brought meat and ale with them to the church, and, after mass, fell to and devoured as much as they possibly could. I confess that I am unable to understand the meaning or the reason of these functions.

I have said little of the Pool. Yet as it is now, so it was then, crowded with craft—of strange build, could we see them with our eyes, but not strange to the boys who looked at the ships, made their way on board, handled the ropes, talked to the sailors, and heard strange stories of men beyond the sea. The Adventurers belonged principally to the Company of Mercers. The owners of the vessels bound to the Levant, to Spain, to Italy, were men well known by name, by sight, and by repute to Dick Whittington. The captains—responsible men, whose lives were continually in peril—were their servants, as were the crews, sturdy bull-dogs all, who might have to fight their way through Moslem pirates of Tripoli, Tunis, Algiers, and Morocco, without counting the Christian corsairs of Italy, Spain, and France. Yet there was safety in the reputation of an English ship, for her sailors would fight. From such talks with such men would a lad of promise and ambition learn such knowledge as would be useful in the coming years —the ports of the known world, the wants of their people, the markets and the supplies. It is quite certain to me that Whittington spent a good deal of his time in the river below Bridge. Perhaps thus he learned the possible value of his cat.

I cannot refrain from quoting one story from Stow which throws a pleasant light on the life of the prentices round Bow Church. It was the duty of the clerk of that church to ring the bell at eight, the signal for knocking off work. The prentices awaited the hour of ringing with a natural impatience. At one time it was discovered that the clerk had fallen into the unpardonable habit of ringing the bell after the time. Was this to be endured ? He received the following warning :—

> " Clerke of the Bow Bell,
>   With the yellow lockes !
> For thy late ringing
>   Thou shalt have knockes."

To which he made haste to reply, with submission :—

> " Children of Chepe,
>   Hold you all stille,
> For you shall have Bow Bell
>   Rung at your wille."

Such, then, was the kind of life into which the boy from Gloucestershire found himself plunged—a life full of excitement, work, joy, amusement of all kinds, discipline, wonder, instruction, and delight—a life which entered into his very soul, and became part of him—so that in after years he could not separate himself, had he wished, from the City of which he became a citizen in his youth.

A lad who came up from the country would see that the people were free ; there were no villains, *ascripti glebæ*, as in his native village ; there was no pride of birth and contempt of obscurity, for all were free men alike, though doubtless it was better to be a mercer than a humble "stringer" or "pelterer." The City was a veritable republic, governed by what seemed to be a freely elected body of officers, who yet were an oligarchy of the richer companies. The people were turbulent, yet lawabiding; they were proud ; they respected themselves and their City ; they regarded the King with a blind loyalty or a pitless animosity, according as he respected their liberties or sought to undermine them ; they were magnificent in their spending ; they loved shows, pageants, great banquets, and splendid apparel ; they were audacious in their enterprises ; they were deeply religious, as in all times has been the English mind ; yet they regarded the monks and priests of their time with contempt very near akin to hatred. Not that they were disposed to the doctrines of Wyclyffe : the good people of London

troubled their heads not one whit about doctrine ;
they loved their splendid churches, their ritual, their
sacred music, but they could not bear the contrast
between the professions of the clergy and their daily
lives. For in that crowded town it was difficult for a
bad priest to conceal his badness.

Again, it was a city in which all the people
were well paid and well fed. The miserable fare
of the country people described by Piers Plowman — their loaves of beans and bran, their
pot-herbs, parsley, cabbages, and fruits—was not
for the Londoners. They lived well on good beef
and mutton, fat capons, and sea fish ; Bordeaux sent
them wine ; for the richer sort wine came, too, from
Gaza in the Holy Land, from Cyprus, from Spain,
from Sicily ; the country districts sent them mead,
perry, and cider. They were a well-fed, prosperous,
and happy people, with certain drawbacks, on which
I have already touched. Among these were, first,
the absence of the habit of bathing—for although the
hot bath was a great mediæval institution, it does not
appear that the middle class used it regularly ; next,
the lack of cleanliness in the streets ; then the lack of
cleanliness, light, ventilation, and space in the houses.
These things were not recognised and regarded as
evils, but they made themselves felt from time to
time in plagues and pestilences. The matter of
cleanliness in all its branches, and with all its

dangers when neglected, set apart, it seems as if London, to a young fellow not yet fully awake to ·the political dangers and the character of the next heir to the throne at the period towards the close of Edward the Third's reign, was, as it is now, the most desirable place of residence upon this terrestrial globe.

And a patriotic City—a City that thought well of itself as the pride and bulwark of England. Was it not well for a lad to come to such a place, to grow up under all its influences, to be fired by its ambitions, to share in its successes, at once to feel the pulse beating and the life-blood of the place surging about him, and to be, himself, a part of all he saw? What sort of life was that led by his brother, Squire of Pauntley, compared with his own? Who could be proud of Pauntley? Whereas, for stately London—

"Stronge be the walls abowte thee that stand,
   Wise be the people that within thee dwelles;
  Fresh is the river with his lusty strand;
   Blithe be thy churches, well sounding are thy bells;
   Rich be thy merchants in substance that excels."

CHAPTER V.

THE STORY OF THE CAT.

"Your tale, sir, would cure deafness."

IN what way and by what steps did Whittington arrive at success? We have read the legendary story of the Cat. It has been long since held up to ridicule by Keightley, and has been explained away by Riley. Nor were there any left who believed that the story was aught but a nursery tale, until Dr. Lysons arose, and with great learning maintained that the story was not only possible, but also probable.

First of all, the same story is related in a dozen different ways and by a dozen different people. Thus, there was one Alphonso, a Portuguese, who, being wrecked on the coast of Guinea, and being presented by the king thereof with his weight in gold for a cat to kill their mice and an ointment to kill their flies, improved the good fortune so rapidly, that within five years he was worth a great sum of money, and after fifteen years' traffic returned to Portugal the

LORD WHITTINGTON AND HIS CAT.

(From an old print.)

third man in the kingdom. Again, the first Spanish cat ever taken to South America was purchased by one Diego Almagro, a companion of Pizarro, for 600 pieces of eight. Arlotto tells the same story in the fifteenth century, when it is also told by the Persian historian named Wassaf; but it was not new in Persia even then, having been told so early as 1219. Tales of the same kind are also found in Denmark and elsewhere.

In fact, so common is the story, that Keightley rejected it at once, as absurd and having no foundation in truth.

"Not at all," says Dr. Lysons; "the very fact of the story being so widely spread, goes to prove that it has some foundation of reality."

He proceeds to show that cats had in some countries a very great value. Thus, an early traveller in South Guinea says, that the cats whose breed come from Europe do not alter in shape and form after generations of liberty in Africa. They are greatly valued by the blacks, he explains, for clearing the houses of rats and mice, which are in those parts very numerous, and do great damage. Indeed, so much mischief was done to the party composing that expedition, that a pound of salt butter was allowed the sailors for every score of rats destroyed. They devoured the parrots alive, stole away the breeches and stockings of the sailors, and bit them severely. Under such circumstances, a cat would indeed be greatly prized. In the middle ages, tame cats were scarce in Europe, and highly valued. Gregory the Great, when he retired to a monastery, took with him nothing but a cat. Mohammed carried about a cat in his sleeve. And at Aix, in Provence, as late as the year 1757, the finest tom-cat that could be procured was carried in procession on *Corpus Christi* day, wrapped in swaddling clothes like a child, and exhibited to the admiration of the multitude in a magnificent shrine. Flowers were strewn and knees were bent before him as he passed. It is said that cats were first brought into Europe from Egypt by way of Cyprus. The skins of cats, moreover, were greatly in demand for the pelisses of abbots and abbesses. All this is no doubt perfectly true. The value of a tame cat and a good mouser was very great, especially in lands where rats and mice abounded. Yet it is difficult to believe that Whittington really made the first step towards his great success by the lucky sale of a cat, confided to a friendly sailor. One would like to know what the cat fetched, and where it was sold, with other circumstances corroborative of the story. Two suggestions have been made to get over the difficulty. They are ingenious, but manifestly impossible. Both are made by Mr. Riley. He thinks that perhaps the word " cat " is a corruption of the French word *achat*, a purchase. And if this will not do, he says that colliers and ships employed in the carriage of sea coal to London were called "cats," so that a "cat" full of coal may have been the foundation of Whittington's fortune.

Let us examine these suggestions. As regards the first, it is perfectly true that the Mercers were retail dealers in the days of Whittington's apprenticeship. They sold most things, and made nothing; they were not a company of handicraftsmen, but of traders; they bought and sold, therefore, whatever money was made was entirely by *achats*, by traffic. Yet the word could not, I think, have been corrupted into "cats." Just as in Scotland, *faché* has become *fashed*, but not *facked*; and *assiette, hashet,* and *gigot, jigot;* so if the word had passed into common use, which it did not, it would have became "ashats" or "ashets." We may therefore dismiss this conjecture.

There remains the second, that he traded with "cats" and sea coal. It is sufficient answer to this that the "cat" was a vessel described or copied from Norwegian models, of burden from five to six hundred tons, and carrying three masts and a bowsprit. Now there is no kind of probability that ships so large were ever built in those days; while the earliest vessels employed in the coal trade were "keels" or "hoys," and the men who worked them were called "keelers." Again, there was a great and very natural prejudice in London against coal fires, on account of their smoke, and its injurious effect. Nor was it until two hundred years later that coal became generally used for manufacturing purposes, but not for domestic use ; and a writer of the time laments the great destruction of woods, because it will lead to the increased use of coal. And Gray (quoted by Lysons) writes in the year 1649 that the coal trade "began not past four score years since." There was, in the fourteenth century, a royal proclamation against the use of coal, as a public nuisance and injurious to the health. Furnaces and kilns erected for the use of coal were ordered to be destroyed. Then, again, supposing all these objections over-ruled, why should Whittington, a mercer, have begun to dabble in an unpopular and an unremunerative trade *outside his own ?* What had merceries to do with coal ? And if any other thing were wanting, how did he raise the money for his first venture in coal ? and why, if he had the money, did he not do as all others of his Company, trade in the legitimate way ?

These arguments appear conclusive. Whittington had no connection with the coal trade, nor is his cat associated with the word *achats.* On the other hand, there used to exist in the Mercers' Hall a portrait of Whittington, dated 1536, in which he is represented, a man of sixty years, in a free livery gown and black cap, having at the left hand a black and white cat. The picture is now lost. The tradition, therefore, is carried back as far as within three generations of Whittington's death. The portrait now in the Mercers' Hall is of later date. Another portrait of Whittington exists, however, by Reginald Elstrack, who flourished about 1590. He is here represented in the robes of Mayor, with a collar of SS, which was introduced in the year 1407 by Henry IV. as his livery; his hand rests upon a cat. The story is told that the hand originally rested on a skull, but that in deference to public opinion a cat was substituted, which proves that the legend, or the history, had been by that time completely spread. That is also proved by a reference to the cat legend in Heywood, "If You Know not Me," and by another in Beaumont and Fletcher's "Knight of the Burning Pestle." The portrait is curious, as showing so striking a resemblance to the contemporary picture representing Whittington on his deathbed, that it seems like a copy, and very likely is. The only reason for supposing that a portrait might have been taken in the lifetime of Whittington is that one of his executors, John Carpenter, Town Clerk of London, was a great patron of painting. It was he, for instance, who caused the North Cloister of St. Paul's to be painted with the Dance of Death.

There are, however, earlier monuments still which connect the great merchant with the cat. The executors of Whittington pulled down and rebuilt

the gaol of Newgate, in conformity with his will.
After the great fire of 1666, we read (Maitland's
"History of London") that the gate of Newgate
was very much damaged:—"The west side of the
gate is adorned with three ranges of Pilasters, and
three entablements of the Tuscan order. Over the
lowest is a circular pediment, and above it the King's
Arms. The outer columns are four niches, with
as many figures as large as life. One of these,
representing Liberty, has carved on his hat the word
Libertas, and the figure of a cat lying at his feet;
alluding to the figure of Sir Richard Whittington, a
former founder, who is said to have made the first step
to his good fortune by a cat." And Pennant states
that Whittington's statue, *with the cat,* remained on
the gate in a niche until the fire. Again, Dr. Lysons
was shown a piece of plate presented to the Mercers'
Company, in the year 1572, by William Burde, then
Warden. "It consists of a gilt car, beautifully chased
and enamelled, standing on four wheels, and bearing
a barrel or tun on the top. There are four medallions in enamel, two on each side: on one of them is
the representation of the Virgin, with a crown, which
are the insignia of the company; on the other, the
arms of the City of London. On the two others are
heraldic cats; while, enamelled in lilac and green, on
the stems of two upright figures, are rats and birds,
the natural food of such animals.'

There is one other fact, and it is a strong one.

The Whittingtons had a house in Gloucester, which they occupied until the year 1460. Now, in the year 1862, this house, then occupied by a draper or mercer, underwent certain repairs, which necessitated excavations in the cellars. There was dug up a stone, .probably part of a chimney, on which, in *basso relievo*, is represented the figure of a boy carrying in his arms a cat. The workmanship appears to be of the fifteenth century. If this is the case, we have a very remarkable proof that the family of Whittington, in his own century—he died in 1423—believed in the cat story.

To sum up, it is clear that the legend cannot be explained away. It is also clear that it was current, and generally believed, certainly in the sixteenth and probably in the fifteenth century; it is nearly certain that the very executors of Whittington, when they rebuilt Newgate, immediately after his death, believed the story; and it would seem that, if his executors wished to commemorate the cat legend, it must have been true.

The case is admirably stated by Dr. Lysons, though in the story which he makes up out of his facts he has thought proper to introduce a good deal from his own imagination. He pictures the boy in tears, giving up his favourite cat reluctantly, parting with the only possession he had in the world with a heavy heart ; and so on.   All this is, of course, pure invention, and it seems a great pity to spoil a good commercial *coup* by false sentiment.   As boys are now, so they were then.   Let us regard Whittington as a healthy, honest lad, who would be no more inclined to cry over a cat than a boy of his age would cry over one now.   And there is one thing very suspicious. If cats were precious, how did he, being so poor as Dr. Lysons would make him, get possession of one? And, seeing how great was the value of a cat in those lands whither the ship was bound, is it unreasonable to suppose that he invested what money he could spare in sending one out for sale?

That I believe to be the real story.   Whittington's first small success was made by a little venture.   The sailors told him about the rats and mice ; he bought a cat, and sent it out.   It was the shrewd venture of a clever boy ; and the cat sold well.   Then he made other ventures, always with profit, and gratefully ascribed his first success to his lucky cat.   That seems to me the only rational way out of the story.

All fortunes, all successes in life, may be traced to a small beginning.   An accident, a word, a gesture, and the after career is changed.   If Dick Whittington shipped a cat for sale, if the cat was sold or bartered for jewels, skins, silk, or ivory, there would be, quite possibly, a first success.

Again, success in anything depends upon the

happy and resolute seizure of opportunities. If a sailor said in the boy's hearing that a cat could be exchanged among the Moors for a large profit, he would be quick enough to go and buy that cat, and entrust his friend to carry it for him, and bring him back honestly what it might fetch—good mousing guaranteed. The cat may just as well have been anything else—a bag of wool, a box of knives, a case of bows and arrows ; the first venture was the first success.

In thus accepting the story of the cat, we do not accept the sentimental rubbish of the legend which Dr. Lysons seemed to think followed with it. The tears of the apprentice, the sacrifice of the one thing which he had to offer, his despair at parting with his favourite, appear to me silly and false. Did one ever hear, in such time of rough and rude sport, when battle and murder were almost daily to be witnessed in the streets of London, of a prentice so far anticipating the future as to weep the sentimental tears of the eighteenth century ? What time had a prentice to cry over his favourite ? what opportunities to keep a favourite at all ? The tears over the cat belong to the same story as the tears of despair on Highgate Hill, the hard taskmaster, the cruel, mocking, teasing fellow-prentices—as if a boy with stuff in him to make him a great and rich merchant was a puling sneak of a boy, not able to give taunt for taunt, or blow for blow!—the want of friends, the neglect of relations, and the penniless condition, all of which may be considered effectually disposed of.

Whittington was the youngest son of a gentleman, though not a rich one. It was not likely, as I have already insisted, that he came up to London a beggar, while his brother was a squire of high degree, afterwards sheriff for his county ; nor did he come up to London seeking a master. He would come, recommended with promises of friendship, to be apprenticed to a Fitz-Warren, a gentleman, *armiger*, of ancient lineage like himself, whose servant he would be for seven years, and afterwards his equal, as being both members of the same Company, albeit one was rich and old, and the other at first poor and young. Then his younger son's portion ; what would he do with that ?

What would every young London merchant do with money? Why, for seven years' apprenticeship the boy had been learning the great lesson that money is made by the right use of money—to sell, one must first buy—and that by selling London merchants become great. He was ready to venture his capital, such as it was ; he did venture it, and he won. Even if he had no money, which I doubt, there is another fact which is of help in showing how young men got on in those days. In the year 1371, a certain John Barnes gave a chest, kept locked with three locks, and having one thousand marks therein, which he devoted to a very novel and praiseworthy use. He had observed that many young men in trade become broken and ruined for want of timely help in the way of a loan, which must not be of an usurious kind. This excellent man, therefore, ordered that sums of money should be taken out of this chest and lent to young men upon sufficient security. For the use thereof, they were to say a *De Profundis* or a *Paternoster*—the very least one could expect of these young men. One need not suppose that Whittington borrowed from this chest-money to buy his cat withal; but the existence of the chest proves that rich merchants were ready to help their younger brethren, and that is a great point to establish. One wonders what became, in the long run, of that chest with the thousand marks.

The story of the cat has been traced to the house of the Whittingtons at Gloucester, sold or let by them in the year 1460; the sculpture of this boy and cat, as any one may see in the Guildhall Museum, is apparently of the fifteenth century. It is also more than probable, almost certain, that the executors of Whittington carved the cat upon the gate of Newgate. We therefore trace it back even to the very life of Whittington. It must have had some origin. The received belief of a great fortune having been made by the sale of a cat is preposterous. It is not, how-

ever, preposterous to believe that a cat was thus sold
for the benefit of young Whittington ; that the first
success, such as it was, encouraged and emboldened
him, so that, for the rest of his life, he always attributed his fortune to the sale of the cat.   And that is
what I am induced to believe is, on the whole, the
true history of the famous cat.

I think that the world is very right to pay worship
and honour to successful men.   When one considers
how, in this realm of England and in the United States,
the very atmosphere is charged with a contagious enthusiasm and zeal for success, so that, above a certain
level, and beyond a certain line of education, there is
hardly a lad who does not look forward with hope to a
life of success, wealth, or fame—though few indeed they
are who get what they desire—and how, further, the
qualities required to ensure success are so many and
so rare, even singly—as, for instance, industry, patience,
cheerfulness, skill in learning, knowledge of man, an
attractive carriage and speech, the power of inspiring
confidence, constant hope, swiftness to seize an opportunity, courage, resolution, self-confidence, which are
only a few—considering these things, I believe we do
well to respect a successful man, and the taunt that
England worships the men who have succeeded
should be accepted as a truthful statement of a practice worthy of defence.   Nor can I see how anything
else is to be greatly admired in a man who fights

the battle of life in the usual way. Whittington, we may be sure, having put his hand to the plough, had no thought of looking back. To be one of the great merchants of London was his ambition. His fortune made, his rank assured, he began to consider (but not till then), as we shall presently see, what he could do with his wealth for the improvement of his city and his fellow-citizens.

CHAPTER VI.

PUBLIC LIFE.

" A merchant was there with a forkèd beard;
In mottely and high on horse he sat:
His reasons spake he full solemnely,
Sounding alway the increase of his winning."

BETWEEN a prentice lad, with all his life before
him for better or for worse, and a rich London
merchant, there is a wide gulf. Unfortunately, in the
case of Whittington, it is impossible, save by conjecture, to bridge it over. As for the story of the
cat, it has been shown that it is not absolutely
impossible ; there are even reasons why it may be
considered possible. And whether it is true in the
main or not, we may safely conjecture that Whittington's success was like that of London merchants in
all ages who make their own way from small ventures
to great—that is to say, there was nothing dramatic
about it, or unexpected. The young man throve
because he possessed the qualities of work, patience,
thrift, and discernment. To all who work honestly
there comes a time of golden chance, which brings

success to him who knows how to take advantage of it. The same virtues which are needed now for success were needed then ; nor does there seem any reason for believing that Whittington's rise was unusually rapid. Thus, on the supposition that he was born about the year 1358, which seems the most probable date, he was just twenty-one years of age when he is first mentioned in the City Records. In 1379 we find him[1] contributing five marks as his share of a loan to the City. Therefore, at twenty-one he had taken up his freedom, and was in trade. This assessment, however, is the lowest of any, though a great many others give the same amount. But John Philpot, the Mayor, is set down for £10, William Walworth, Nicolas Brembre, and others for £5 each. So that here we have a proof that, in the year 1379, Whittington was as yet only on the first step of Fortune's ladder, and was certainly not considered richer than the general run of London traders. However, the year marks a kind of commencement to his public life. Henceforth for forty years he is a part of the civic history, taking his share in maintaining the City rights and forwarding the City interests.

It was while Whittington was passing out of his apprenticeship that the City petitioned the King against certain rights of importation and sale which

---

[1] Riley's " Memorials," p. 534.

K

had been granted to foreigners. The City has always been jealous, up to late years, of foreign merchants. And to one who bought and sold stuffs as Whittington dealt with, the question was one of very great importance. A charter obtained in 1376 prevented foreigners from selling by retail. This prohibition would work in two ways to the advantage of the Mercers and "Adventurers;" for whatever the foreign merchants imported, they could only sell to the London merchants wholesale, so that the latter could fix their own price, and there was nothing to prevent them from making it so low as to drive foreign ships out of the port altogether. This, no doubt, was what they intended and wished to do. London for the Londoners was the first thing. The City had not yet become the market of the world, open to all comers. Foreign influences, however, were strong at Court, and in the household of Prince Richard. The citizens therefore determined on giving a great entertainment to the Prince, with a view of conciliating him. He was living in 1377, just before the death of his grandfather, at Kennington Palace with the Princess his mother. They organised, therefore, a great *chevauché*, consisting of 130 citizens, among whom, one hopes, young Whittington was permitted to ride. They were all on horseback, and rode from Newgate, over London Bridge, to Kennington, preceded by flambeaux and a band of music. They were not dressed in their usual civic and company liveries, but impersonated Esquires, Knights, Pope, Cardinals, and Devils. Try to picture the procession. First the trumpets, fifes, and drums, with other instruments of strange appearance and sound ; then the men carrying the torches, to be lit at nightfall ; then the Esquires, gallant and brave, with arms and shields ; then the Knights in shining armour and with flying banners ; then the Pope—actually the Pope !—followed by his Cardinals and his Devils, the latter indicating, by their diabolical activity and their gestures, a greedy desire to carry off the spectators then and there to their own quarters. The Prince appears to have thought the procession most magnificent. After the march past, the leaders of the Riding proposed to the Prince a throw with dice. These were loaded, so that his Highness might always win. By this crafty device they managed to make him accept a bowl, a cup, and a ring, all of gold. Similar presents were made to his mother and to the people of her suite, and then they lit up their torches and rode home again, followed no doubt by all the prentice boys.

The story is remarkable, because it shows how dependent upon royal favour was this city, great and strong as it was already—so strong that it seems to us, considering the rest of the realm, how weak it was, and how open to attack at many points, that

London had only to close her gates and defy the
Sovereign. No doubt she could have done so at any
time, and successfully, had all her people been of one
mind. But they remained loyal while it was in the power
of law-loving men to be loyal, and the time had not
come when men should think any government even possible without a lawful king. All this childish acting to
please a prince ! Yet no doubt it served its purpose.
Unfortunately, the good effects of the procession and
the golden gifts were marred by the untoward quar-
relling and brawl at the trial of Wycliffe, in the same
year. He had been summoned by the Archbishop of
Canterbury and the Bishop of London to appear
before them at St. Paul's Cathedral, there to answer
to whatever charges might be brought against him.
This meant, in the case of an unprotected priest,
deprivation and imprisonment. But Wycliffe was not
unprotected. He came not alone, but accompanied
by John of Gaunt, Duke of Lancaster, and Lord
Piercy, Marshal of England. A quarrel arose between
the Duke and the Bishop of London, who was indignant that a heretic should receive such protection.
The Duke threatened to drag the Bishop out of the
church by the hair of his head. The speech was
reported to the mob outside, who shouted that they
would all die before any indignity was offered to
their Bishop. John of Gaunt, in that kind of rage
which used to be called royal, went to the Parliament,

then sitting, and proposed that the office of Mayor should be abolished, and the Marshal of England be empowered to make arrests and hold his court in the City. It shows how deeply the Londoners were penetrated with pride in their liberties and institutions, to read that they rose in tumult on a report of the Duke's proposal, and, after plundering the Marshalsea, rushed to the Savoy, his palace, and would have sacked and destroyed it, but for the intervention of the Bishop of London.

This looked like the loss of Court favour altogether ; and, though the Mayor and Aldermen made haste to represent to the King that the riot was a popular commotion only, which they had done their best to suppress, they were commanded to wait upon the King—then on the point of death at Shene—were reprimanded, and dismissed their posts. Nicolas Brembre, a citizen personally devoted to John of Gaunt, was appointed Mayor, and the animosity of the Duke was appeased by the young King. When he rode into the City, accompanied by his uncles, and all were entertained by the Mayor and Aldermen, the wound was completely healed, and it seemed as if Richard II. was resolved to maintain the liberties and charters of the City. In the end, it was worse for him that he did not.

In the same year there was a scare about the insecure and unguarded position of the ships in the river. It was ordered that four aldermen should always be on board the outer ships, both day and night, " to avoid perils which might ensue to the shipping of the Thames, to the irreparable loss and damage of the whole nation." They were to be accompanied by a sufficient number of men-at-arms. It is not stated how long this precauti n was maintained.

In the year 1378 the most patriotic office ever accomplished by any citizen was rendered to the City of London by John Philpot, then Mayor. For some time the navigation of the Channel and the North Sea had been greatly impeded and annoyed by the depredations of a certain Scottish pirate or privateer, named Mercer, who had a small fleet of ships, with which he assailed and destroyed the English merchantmen. Petitions and remonstrances addressed to the Crown produced no effect. Then this excellent citizen, Sir John Philpot, resolved to end the thing at once, equipped a fleet at his own sole expense and charge, manned his ships with a thousand stout fellows, fully armed, put himself on board as captain—saw one ever a more valiant Mayor?—and sailed forth in pursuit of the enemy. He found Pirate Mercer off Scarborough, embarrassed with his prizes, which he was loath to quit, but which divided his forces, and made him fight at a disadvantage. While he was pondering which were better, Sir John fell upon him

with all his valiant Londoners, utterly routed and
discomfited him, slew him and most of his men, and
presently returned to the Nore with all his ships,
most of his men, and the Scottish pirate's ships,
including fifteen Spanish ships which had joined
him ; so that there was great rejoicing, especially
in the Mercers' Company, and among all who had
ventures afloat and were owners of ships.   True that
the King's Highness could not tolerate that war
should be made upon any without his permission
and consent, and Sir John must needs go before
the Court and explain his presumption.   I know
not what he said, but the case was clear.   So many
enemies of London trade swept off the seas ; the
ships now able to set sail without fear of wolves.
Were the King's coffers likely soon to want re-
plenishment ?   In fact, before another year was
over there was great need of money in the royal
treasury.   Then Sir John Philpot came once more to
the rescue.   The arms and armour of a thousand men
lay in pawn ; Sir John took them out.   The King
wanted ships for his expedition to France ; Sir
John gave him all those ships of his own which
had already done for Mercer.   Here was an example,
if example were wanted, for a young merchant.
What nobler Mayor to set before his eyes than this
brave Sir John ?

There is no mention of Whittington's name in

any of these doings, nor in that great and perilous rising of the peasants in the year 1381 ; but we cannot expect that a young man just beginning to trade would have any chance of distinction. Enough for him to obey commands, and to fight on the side of freedom. One knows not how far the socialist teachings of John Ball, with his verses of " Jack the Miller," " Jack the Carter," and " Jack Trewman," influenced the craftsmen of the City. It is, however, noteworthy that no resistance was offered to the mob which rushed over London Bridge, and for awhile took possession of the City. The Savoy, the Temple, and the houses of the foreign merchants (the last must have been the work of the London craftsmen) were burned, without any attempt made to resist the rebels. The Archbishop of Canterbury and the Prior of St. John were dragged to Tower Hill and beheaded ; but no one moved. The slaying of Wat Tyler by Sir William Walworth was clearly unpremeditated, and an act of uncontrollable rage ; besides, Walworth had lost many houses in the general mischief. Yet, when a rumour ran that the young King's life was in danger, an army of 6,000 Londoners was formed at a moment's notice to rally round their Sovereign. These would be Londoners of the better sort ; one fears that among the poor artizans the questions had been asked, and had sunk deep into their hearts--" Will things ever

Death of Wat Tyler.

go well so long as things be not in common? Why
are we poor, and why are they rich?" They asked
themselves the same question in the year 1381 which
millions are asking themselves exactly five hundred
years later. It is an ominous question; when it is
asked often and persistently it bodes mischief, because
no one has yet found such an answer as will make
poor men contented with their poverty.

As for Whittington, however, one cannot doubt
that he was in arms with that troop of 6,000
armed citizens, stout men all and true, who turned
out to follow their Mayor and defend their King.

Whittington's birth and connections allied him to
the party of those who possessed, rather than to that
which desired to possess. For that reason, it is
probable that he was not carried away with the
Lollardry which had now infected the lower classes
of the country. We shall have something to say,
presently, on Whittington's religious opinions; meantime, it is sufficient to remark that the earlier years
of his freedom were marked with many civic troubles
and tumults.

Foremost among the discontented was one John
of Northampton, Mayor in 1381 and 1382, who, like
William Longbeard, seems to have been a Reformer
and a Radical before his time. That is to say, if a
thing seemed desirable, he carried it out with absolute
disregard to the enemies he might be making and the

prejudices he was attacking. For instance, it certainly was the province of the Ecclesiastical Courts to look after the morality of the City. It was not denied by any that these courts allowed scandals to exist which could easily have been suppressed ; the officers either connived or took bribes. Yet it was a bold step of the Mayor to take over to himself the authority of these courts, and to purify the City in spite of bishop and clergy. Nor was it a measure likely to secure the affection of the clergy, when the same John gave order that the parish priests should be forbidden to take fees above a certain amount : not more, for instance, than the fourth part of a silver penny—and a simple fat capon not to be had under three pence— for a mass for the dead ; nor more than forty pence —which seems a pretty round sum as prices then went—for the baptism of a child ; nor for a marriage more than half-a-mark or the value thereof. It is not lucky to attack the Church ; and though good citizens might feel that John of Northampton meant well, and was acting in their interests, his quarrels with the fishmongers, which followed, and proved his destruction, were no doubt considered by his enemies as a judgment. It will be remembered that Chaucer, Controller of Customs, belonged to the party of John of Northampton.

The sale of fish in the City has always been a most important branch of trade, and the fishmongers have on several occasions proved a troublesome body to deal with. In the fourteenth century, though the moral authority of the Church was small, its authority in the matter of fasts was absolute. On fast days the whole nation fasted. On every Friday throughout the year, all through Lent, and on many fast days besides, the world of Christendom lived upon fish. There was fresh fish and preserved fish. The people who lived inland had rivers, tanks, and ponds ; those near the shore had sea fish. The Londoners commanded access to the sea, and a very large demand existed for fresh and good fish. For about a quarter of the whole year, in fact, they had to live chiefly upon it. Therefore, it was above all things important that the people should be well and cheaply provided. An abundant and inexhaustible supply was to be found in the lower Thames, off the coasts of Kent, Suffolk, and Norfolk. The retail of the fish brought to Billingsgate and Queenhithe was entirely in the hands of the Fishmongers' Company. In an evil moment for himself, John of Northampton became a Free Trader, and obtained an act of Parliament whereby the whole trade of fish, both retail and wholesale, was thrown open to foreigners as well as Londoners, and the occupation, calling, mystery, or craft of the fishmongers declared to be no true craft or mystery, and unworthy to be reckoned among those for which the Livery Companies were

established.   This was a very strong step, considering
the vested interests of the fishmongers; but John
of Northampton did not stop there.   He endeavoured
to extend his Free Trade principles, and, having
thrown down the barriers of protection for fish, he
began to attack the vested interests of other purveyors.   He showed his intention by first procuring
another Act of Parliament, by which victuallers of all
kinds were debarred from holding any judicial office
in the City.   Grocers, butchers, pepperers, fruiterers,
bakers, were therefore about to be included with the
fishmongers, and the Reformer would proceed to
nothing less than a general massacre, so to speak, in
which the fortunes of all concerned with the pro-
visioning of London would be wrecked.   But things
were not yet ripe for measures so drastic.

Protection was to reign for many years to come;
and it is sad to record how the Reformer, born before
his time, came to grief.   For Sir Nicolas Brembre,
himself destined to illustrate in a striking manner the
uncertainty of fortune, being made Mayor again, restored the fishmongers to their former liberties.   Thereupon fish went up in price, and there was some kind
of tumult, headed, unhappily, by John of Northampton himself, and by one Constantyn, who was daring
enough to shut up his shop, and to call upon his
fellow-citizens to do the like.   Thereupon they lost
no time in cutting off his head.   As for poor John of

Northampton, he was sent away to the Castle of
Tintagel, on the Cornish coast, where, amid the
everlasting beat of the Atlantic at his feet, the crying
of the sea-gulls, and the roar of the wind, which in
that vexed peninsula is never still, he was able, to the
end of his days, to reflect upon the folly of being a
Free Trader before the time was ripe. Let us pray to
be delivered from ideas too much in advance of our
time—a little, and yet a little, before our fellows, so
that we may go in front, and lead the way, and reap
immortal glory for our prescience, but not too much !

It is remarkable that the first entry made in the
English language in the City Letter-books refers to
this sedition, and prohibits popular gatherings In
the year 1384, a reform was effected in the election
of the Common Council, which hitherto had been
chosen from the companies and crafts, but without
any strict rule as to number ; and it was complained
that many things were passed in " clamour "—that is,
without due consideration — for want of sufficient
persons. It was now, however, ordained that henceforth the Common Council should be chosen from
the wards " fifteen days after St. Gregory," and that
it should be summoned once a quarter, or oftener, to
deliberate over the affairs of the City. The immediate result of this action would probably tend to
increase the power of the great companies, because
only the richer and more eminent citizens—that is,

those who belonged to a trade rather than a handicraft — would wish to join the Council. It was also, doubtless, owing to this change that Whittington himself was elected in the following year one of the Common Council for Coleman Street Ward. During his year of office there occurred one of those disputes which were constantly being caused by the encroachments of the Crown. In this case the King ordered that the sheriffs should be sworn before the Barons of the Exchequer, instead of before the Mayor and Aldermen, as belonged to the rights of the City. The Mayor protested, but the Crown, for this time, carried the point.

When the troubles of the new reign fairly set in, it is remarkable to observe that the first to take any steps for the better administration of the country were the citizens of London. In the great deputation which was sent to the King at Windsor, one of the deputies boldly told Richard that justice was never less practised in England than at that time, and that by the subtlety and craft of certain persons it was not possible for the King to come at the truth of things. It was, again, an army of Londoners which, under the Duke of Gloucester, defeated the Duke of Ireland at Oxford. They opened their gates to the Baron's army, and delivered up their late Mayor, Sir Nicolas Brembre, who had incurred suspicion of being one of the King's favourites, to be executed at Tyburn.

Read also, to prove the power of the Londoners, Froissart's account of the capture of the King by the Duke of Lancaster :—

"When the army was within two miles of Flint they came to a village, where they halted, and the Earl (Henry of Lancaster) refreshed himself with meat and drink. He there resolved, in his own mind, without consulting others, to march with only two hundred horse, leaving the rest behind, and when nearing the castle where the King was, to endeavour, by fair speeches, to enter the castle, and cajole the King to come forth and trust to him, who would insure him against all perils on his road to London, engaging that he should not suffer any bodily harm, and promising to mediate between him and the Londoners, who were greatly enraged against him. . . . . . . The King, on seeing him, changed colour, as one who knew that he had greatly misconducted himself. The Earl spoke loud, without paying any reverence or honour to the King, and asked him, 'Have you broken your fast?' The King replied, 'No; it is yet early morn. Why do you ask?' . . . Then the King washed his hands, seated himself at table, and was served. They asked the Earl if he would not be seated and eat. He said, 'No; for he had breakfasted.' During the time the King was eating (which was not long, for his heart was too much oppressed for eating), the whole country was covered with men-at-arms and archers, who could be plainly seen from the windows of the castle. The King, on rising from the table, perceived them, and asked his cousin the Earl who they were. He replied, 'For the most part Londoners.' 'And what do they want?' said the King. 'They want to take you,' answered the Earl, ' and carry you to the Tower of London ; and there is not any means of pacifying them unless you consent to go.' ' No !' replied the King, who was much frightened at hearing this, for he knew the Londoners hated him ; and continued, 'cannot you, cousin, prevent this ? I would not willingly yield myself into their hands, for I am aware they hate me, and have done so for a long time, though I am their Sovereign.' The Earl answered, ' I see no other way to prevent it.' "

To this story must be added the fact that Richard, in spite of the bad government of his later years, had endeared himself to many of the citizens by his good government during those years which followed his taking over the reins of power. The illegal exactions, the encroachments, the taxes, which drove London into revolt, and armed Henry of Bolingbroke with the strength of their money and men, could not make some of them forget the handsome, brave boy who stood fearless before the mob of peasants, nor the King who reigned for nine years justly and by counsel of Parliament. When, thirty years later, Whittington founded his college, his priests were enjoined to pray not for Henry the Fourth, whom London made King, but for Richard the Second, whom London had deposed—the gallant Prince of his youth.

Whittington's name is found again, in 1387, as one of the Common Council for Coleman Street Ward. In 1389 he is named as becoming surety to the

Chamberlain for the sum of £10 towards the defence of the City. We may remark that it is ten years since we find him assessed at five marks against the £10 of Sir John Philpot. These ten years were surely very prosperous, seeing that in so short a time Whittington had risen from an assessment of five marks to that of ten pounds; that is to say, to the level of the richest citizens. He was now probably about thirty-one years of age, but though his wealth increases, his fellow-citizens do not hastily impose civic honours upon him ; nor is it until the year 1393, when he was, in our supposition, thirty-five years old, that he is chosen an Alderman. It was for Broad Street Ward, and in the same year he was elected Sheriff. Fortunately for him he did not receive this honourable and dangerous distinction the preceding year, which was marked by another royal invasion of the City Charters. On various pretexts, the Mayor, the Sheriffs, and the Aldermen were all arrested. They were fined ; the liberties of the City were seized ; and to get them restored, the citizens had to pay a fine of 3,000 marks. Patience appeared to be the only remedy, as yet. The City, after paying the fine, showed its desire to recover the royal favour by receiving King and Queen with a great pageant and costly presents. The lamb might as well try to conciliate the wolf. Richard the Second had passed through the phase of parliamentary

L

government to absolute rule. He was always in want of money; the City appeared to him to be always full of money. Should he, a King, suffer from an empty purse when burgesses went rich? What were charters when the treasury was bare? It was a dangerous thing in this reign to hold a city office; justice, respect to charters, was there none; no trust could be placed in the King or his advisers; many of the richest citizens, perhaps Whittington among them, were forced to sign and seal blank charts, to be afterwards filled up by the King's ministers. Can we picture to ourselves the agony and anxiety consequent upon the signing of a blank cheque, the amount to be filled in at pleasure by the Chancellor of the Exchequer?

Yet Whittington was in the City to bear scot and lot, and it fell to his lot, in the year 1397, to take the place of Adam Bamme, Mayor, who died in his year of office. The few months during which he acted in place of Bamme are by some reckoned a year of Mayoralty. At the conclusion of the year he was elected Mayor for the following year. His election was conducted with so much clamour—city politics running high at the time, as they well might, considering those blank charts—that a change was made in the mode of election. No one, henceforth, was to be present at an election except the Mayor, Sheriffs, and Aldermen.

His first year of office passed in comparative quiet : however much the merchants might have been robbed, there was no arresting of the City officers. But when Henry of Lancaster landed at Ravenspur, the patience of London was exhausted, and the City received him with open arms, supplying him with all kinds of provisions.

His accession to the Crown gave the greatest satisfaction to the people of London ; they had once more a King who understood the importance of conciliating them, encouraging their trade, and respecting their charters. The great free town, loyal, rich, and powerful, was an auxiliary of greater importance than the adhesion of half the Barons of England. Henry assigned seats at his coronation banquet to the Mayor and Aldermen, as, in their collective capacity, the official Chief Butler of England. He further gratified them by providing that the magistrates of the City, in default of good government, should be tried by a commission taken out of the counties of Kent, Essex, Sussex, Hereford, Buckingham, and Berks. To show their gratitude, the City turned out an army of 6,000 men, all fully armed, to march with the King on the threat of an invasion. In the year 1401, water was brought from Tyburn to Cornhill in leaden pipes.

In the year 1406, Whittington was elected **Mayor**, in succession to John Woodcock, for the second

time. The manner of his election is thus described
(Riley's " Memorials ")—

"John Wodecok, Mayor, considering that upon the
Feast of the Translation of St. Edward the King and
Confessor (vol. vi. 10), he and all the Aldermen of the said
city, and as many as possible of the wealthier and more substantial Commoners of the same city, ought to meet at the
Guildhall, to elect a new Mayor for the ensuing year,
ordered that a Mass of the Holy Spirit should be celebrated
with solemn music in the Chapel annexed to the said Guildhall, to the end that the same Commonalty might be able,
peacefully and amicably, to nominate two able and proper
persons to be Mayors of the said city for the ensuing year,
by favour of the clemency of our Saviour, according to the
customs of the said city.

This was accordingly done, and the commoners " peacefully and amicably, without any clamour or discussion, did
becomingly nominate Richard Whytyngton, mercer, and
Drew Barentyn, goldsmith, through John Westone, com
mon Countor of the said city, and presented the same.
And hereupon the Mayor and Alderman, with closed doors,
in the same chamber chose Richard Whytyngton aforesaid,
by the guidance of the Holy Spirit, to be Mayor of the City
for the ensuing year."

The following years were, on the whole, a time of
great prosperity and peace to the City, and, no doubt,
to Whittington himself. In the year 1406 he was
elected Mayor for the second time, and in 1419 for
the third time. In 1416 he was returned Member of
Parliament for the City.

It was no new or unusual thing in those days for a man to serve as Mayor, and in earlier times a man was sometimes Mayor for several years in succession. In the reign of Edward III., for instance, we find that Loufkin, Pounteney, and Brembre (the same who was afterwards executed for being one of Richard's favourites) were each four times Mayor; Aubrey and Hammond were each elected Mayor three times; Leggy, Francis, Bury, Burns, Walworth, Exton, and Northampton, each twice.

As regards the functions, hospitalities, and pageants in which Whittington took part during those years, these were many and magnificent. First of all, there were the *chevauchés*—the Ridings—of the newly-elected Mayors. In these great processions, of which the modern survival is but a mockery, the Companies turned out, court, members, prentices, and serving-men, the first on horseback, the rest on foot, in their colours and with their banners; they were preceded by minstrels,[1] and the streets were hung with tapestry. The Water Procession did not begin until the reign of Henry VI. Next there were the usual Companies' festivities, and then the extraordinary ceremonies.

---

[1] In the *chevauchés* of Walcot (1401) we find that 40 shillings were paid for minstrels, of whom there were only six; this seems a great deal for a single day, but perhaps the amount included pay for other work. The beadle got fourpence for the hire of a horse; eightpence was paid for " Cheprons and Fessures."

Thus, in the year 1401, came Emanuel Palæologus, seeking assistance against the Turks. The Emperor Sigismund was another illustrious visitor in 1415. There was a great tournament between the gentlemen of Hainault and those of England, held at Smithfield. There was a splendid Passion play acted at Skinner's Well, near Clerkenwell, by a company of parish clerks. The Prince of Wales came to live in the City in the year 1480, taking the great house in Thames Street known as Cold Herbergh—*i.e.*, Cold Harbour. No doubt Sir John Falstaff, Poins, and others of the Prince's private friends came with him, and lights were seen in the windows of Cold Herbergh late o' nights. In the year 1415 there was such a rejoicing in the City as was not afterwards witnessed for exactly four hundred years to come. Happy the prentice boy who saw that day! It was fortunately on Lord Mayor's Day; surely such a Lord Mayor's Day, with such a splendid surprise, was never seen before, and perhaps will never be known again. On the 13th of October, Sir Nicolas Wotten was elected Mayor for the ensuing year in the Chapel of the Guildhall, and sworn on the Feast of Saint Simon and Saint Jude—viz., October 28th. For several days the City had been agitated by rumours of defeat and disaster in France, and on the 29th, when the usual march was to be made to Westminster, all hearts were heavy with gloomy apprehensions. But lo! while he was riding on the way, there was brought to the Mayor the great and joyful intelligence of Agincourt. He rode on to take the oath, and there, accompanied by the Bishop of Winchester, the Lord High Chancellor, and other great officers, he proceeded to Paul's, and assisted at a *Te Deum*. The next day there was a grand procession. It marched on foot, in token of humility, from St. Paul's to Westminster, where the solemn thanksgiving of the nation was offered for the King's successes; and on the following day another and a grander procession was made on horseback from Westminster to Paul's. Then came the King's return, with the greatest "Riding" ever known, to receive him, his plunder, and his prisoners. Lydgate describes it at length—

> " The Mayor of London was redy bown
>   With all the craftes of that cite ;
> All clothed in red throughout the town,
>   A seemely sight it was to see.

> " To the Blakheth thanne rode he,
>   And spredde the way on either side :
> XX^teM men might well see
>   Our comely Kyng for to abyde."

It was in the year 1400 that England, to her shame and dishonour, began to burn people who ventured to use their reason, and to deny the unreasonable. The great body of Londoners, ignorant, and fond of the ecclesiastical shows, were profcundly orthodox. There is no reason to suppose that the better class were otherwise, else we should hear of some of them also being burned for their opinions. There is nothing whatever to show that Whittington ever swerved from the obedience to Church which he had learned as a youth. The first who suffered was William Sawtre, parish priest of St. Osyth ; ten years later, John Bradby, a tailor, was burned for holding Wycliffe's opinions. The Prince of Wales was present, and after the execution began he ordered the wretched man to be taken out and offered pardon if he would recant ; but he stoutly refused, and so was put back again, and died.

In 1415, John Cleyden, a carrier, was burned for the same offence.

In 1416 the City was first lighted at night ; the citizens were ordered to hang lanterns over their doors, but the rules were stringent against those who were found in the streets after dark.

In 1407 a plague visited London, and carried off 30,000 persons.

In 1419, one of the earliest of the many benevolent institutions of London was founded by Sir Thomas Eyre, who built Leadenhall, as a place in which should be constantly kept a great store of grain, in case of a public famine. Whittington had already opened Bakewell Hall, which stood on the site of the present Guildhall Buildings, for the sale of broad-cloths. In order to avoid " disorderly and deceitful bargainings" between foreign drapers and London freemen, it was ordered that all goods of this kind should be exposed in the hall from Thursday to Saturday, and then to be sold. There was little enough of " freedom of contract" in those days. Whittington's creed was, that men's inclinations are evil, and that it was better to prevent rogueries than to punish them. Perhaps some day we shall revert to the old methods.

In the year 1410 the new Guildhall was commenced, on a site east of the old hall. Two years later an ordinance was passed, in which, after stating that the work had stopped through failure of support and " helping hands," it was enacted (1) that every apprentice should pay, for the furtherance of the building, a fee of two shillings and sixpence on entrance ; (2) that at the close of his time he should pay three shillings and fourpence ; (3) that a fine, to be agreed upon, should be paid by every person purchasing the freedom of the City ; (4) that for the enrolment of every deed should be paid three shillings and fourpence ; (5) for the enrolment of every will the sum of six shillings and eightpence ; (6) for every letter patent, the sum of two shillings ; (7) for every letter sealed by the Mayor, twelvepence above the

former fees ; (8) that all victuallers' fines and the
fines of the Mayor's Court should be appropriated
to the work ; (9) that for six years the sum of 100
marks should annually be taken from the revenues
of London Bridge ; and (10) that all defaulters in
their ward motes should pay a fine of fourpence.

The City records make mention of two or three
official acts of Whittington which are of less importance, but help to throw light upon the manners of the
time. Thus, in the year 1418, at a general Court
held at the Guildhall, Whittington being present
among the aldermen, it was agreed that the chaplain
of the Chapel over the Bones of the Dead in St.
Paul's Churchyard, " who had exposed himself to
manifold and constant anxieties for the good and
honour of the Chapel aforesaid," should yearly be
presented, on Christmas Day, with a gown of the
same suit or livery as that given to the sergeants
of the Mayor. This does not seem liberal, but
clothes in those days were not changed every season.

In the same year one Johanna, wife of Rothewel of
Hendon, fell into trouble for defaming Richard
Whittington—saying that he owed her large sums
of money, and that he had jewels and goods of hers
to the value of many thousand marks. She had to
confess in open court that the charge was false and
libellous, because, in truth, she owed the said Richard
Whittington more than he owed her ; and she begged

for mercy. Here the case ends abruptly, but we can have no doubt that the clemency which I have already remarked upon as common among the City magistrates was not withheld in the case of this woman, who would otherwise have been paraded through the town, and placed in the Thewe, with a whetstone about her neck, to signify that she was a liar.

In his third year of office, Whittington issued a proclamation against the mixture and adulteration of wines, and punished with pillory one William Horold, who had placed certain gums and spices in casks, then filled them with "old and feeble" Spanish wine, "to have a lykly manere taste and smell to the drynkyng of Romeny" — that is, Malmsey — and would then have sold the same.

In the same year, before Whittington's election, a very singular step was taken. The preamble of the ordinance explains the case :—

"Whereas the commendable intentions and charitable purpose of those who have been governors and presidents of the City of London heretofore have ordained a prison, called Ludgate, for the good and comfort of poor freemen of the said city who have been condemned, to the end that such poor prisoners might, more freely than others who are strangers, dwell in quiet in such place, and pray for their benefactors, and live upon the alms of the people. . . . Now, from one day to another, the charitable intentions and commendable purposes aforesaid are frustrated and turned to evil, inasmuch as many false persons, of bad

disposition and purpose, have been more willing to take up
their abode there, so as to waste and spend their goods
upon the ease and licence that there is within, than to pay
their debts; and, what is even more, do therein compass,
conspire, and imagine oftentimes, through others of their
false covin, to indict good and loyal men for felonies and
treasons of which they have never been guilty."

In other words, freemen of the City chose rather to
live in the gaol of Ludgate, on the alms provided for
poor prisoners, than to work and pay their debts;
and, worse still, they made use of their time to get up
conspiracies against honourable citizens. The only
remedy that could be devised was to move all the
prisoners to Newgate, and close the gaol. This was
done in the month of June, but in November, Richard
Whittington being Mayor, it was found that most of
the wretches taken to Newgate had died there, " by
reason of the foetid and corrupt atmosphere;" whereupon Ludgate was reopened, " seeing that every
person is bound to support and be tender of the
lives of men."

It was in this his last mayoralty that Whittington
entertained Henry of Agincourt and his Queen. The
magnificence of this banquet astonished both the
King and his bride; probably there was not, in all
England and France together, another man who
could have provided such a banquet. For, although
there were great nobles, with a vast territory and

Newgate Prison.

many thousands of vassals, there was not certainly, outside the City of London, any one who could command the rich and splendid things which were ready to the hand of a great merchant. Even the fires were fed with cedar and perfumed wood. When Catherine spoke of it, the Mayor proposed to feed the flames with something still more costly and valuable ; and, in fact, he threw into the fire the King's own bonds, to the amount of £60,000. Among the bonds were some, to the amount of 10,000 marks, due to the Mercers' Company ; one of 1,500 marks, due to the Chamber of London ; one of 2,000 marks, belonging to the Grocers ; and all Whittington's private loans and advances. It is probable that in burning these bonds the Mayor acted by previous agreement of the City ; but if not—if he took on himself the loans due to the Companies—he made a most splendid and princely gift. The sum of £60,000 advanced by one man would, even in these days, be considered enormous ; in those days it can hardly be reckoned as less than a million and a quarter of our present money. Did the Patriotic Fund, the contribution of a whole nation, amount to more ? A simple way of reckoning is to remember that, as we have seen (p. 120), the board of a girl among respectable people was reckoned at eightpence a-week. On the most moderate computation, three times that sum

would now be asked per diem ; so that the cost
of living is multiplied by twenty-one, which makes
the gift more than a million and a quarter.   The
man who would sacrifice so much must have been
very patriotic, as well as very rich.

The busy life was now drawing to a close ; the
few remaining years of the great citizen seem to
have been chiefly spent in devising means by which
he might benefit the city which he loved.   Of these
means we shall speak in the next chapter.   We have
one more glimpse of him in his old age.   He is no
longer in office, but he prosecutes certain tradesmen
for overstepping the limits of their trade.   They are
fined ; yet when the old man, his business done, goes
away, the clerk of the court gets up and goes too.
" How then ?   We have not yet paid the fine."
No ; nor do they pay it.   For the sentence was passed
only to please old Sir Richard.   This makes one feel
as if, when he was gone, there would be one the less
to testify for justice and to stand up for truth.

It is one proof of the consideration in which Whittington was held in these his later years, that when
Henry the Fifth was about to repair Westminster
Abbey, he would have none of the work taken in hand
until Whittington had seen and approved the plans.

The end, as we shall see, came in the year 1423,
when Whittington, according to my reckoning, was
sixty-five years of age.

CHAPTER VII.

PRIVATE LIFE AND BENEFACTIONS.

"By a writing in this man's owne hand, it appeareth what a pitifull and relenting heart he had at other men's miseries."

HOLINSHED.

LET us, finally, endeavour to pourtray the man in his private capacity. We know, perhaps, more than would be believed possible of one concerning whom no antiquarian up to the day of Dr. Lysons troubled himself to investigate. And what is known of him is a splendid monument to the patience, the sagacity, and the knowledge shown by the antiquary who, by great good fortune, was led to take up the subject.

Whittington married Alice, daughter of his master, Sir John Fitz-Warren. It is not known in what year the marriage took place, but, as will be seen immediately, there is every reason to believe that his success began early in life, and therefore we are justified in supposing that he married young. The fact of his marrying the daughter of the man with whom he had been a prentice also points to a pretty little idyll of love, of which one would like to know more. But, as we have seen already, it was not the marriage of a low-born country lad with the daughter of a wealthy merchant. Whittington was an equal in birth with his wife, and both belonged to gentle-folk.

It appears that in the year 1386, when he was already not more than twenty-eight years of age, Whittington lent his maternal uncle, Philip Mansel, the sum of £500 sterling, taking as security the title-deeds of Lippicote, in Gloucestershire. From this it is clear—the amount representing at least £5,000 of our money—that his success must have been rapid and early, and there is no reason to doubt that he would feel justified in marrying before this date. He had no children, and was apparently left a widower some years before his death. His arms (see p. 31) are impaled with those of the Fitz-Warrens in the church of Pauntley, which shows that he was anxious to show his connection with his own kith and kin.

He is said to have lived in Hart Street, four doors from Mark Lane, and his house, called Whit-tington Palace, was standing, though in a dilapidated condition, in the year 1796, when it was described by a correspondent in the "Gentleman's Magazine." A drawing of the house is also given. The description of the house is as follows :—

" It then formed three parts of a square, that is to say, it was built, like so many great houses of the period, in the stately fashion, round a court. The fourth side of the court probably consisted of a wall and a gate, unless at first that side also was enclosed. The great houses of London merchants in those days were probably all built round courts; the old taverns still remaining are examples of this mode of building. Under the windows of the first story were carved, in *basso-relievo*, the arms of the Twelve Companies of London, except one, destroyed to make room for a cistern. The wings were supported by rude carved figures, representing Satyrs. The principal room was twenty-five feet long, fifteen feet broad, and ten feet high. It had a wainscot six feet high, and carved, over which were a continuation of Saxon arches in *basso-relievo*, and between each arch a human figure. The ante-room has nothing worth notice but the mantelpiece, which, however, is much more modern than the outside, as is the adjoining room, which belongs to a basket-maker. It is not quite so large as the principal room, but the ceiling is as superbly decorated with carving. On a tablet is the date 1609, and on another are the initials M. M. P. This room appears to have been fitted up long since the building of the house. In medallions on the above ceiling are several heads of the Cæsars, and two coats of arms—a chevron between nine pallets—but no colours are expressed."

The house, in fact, was an ancient house of the better kind, built round a court. When it was pulled down, in the beginning of this century, a singular discovery was made. There was found in the basement

M

a small brick-built chamber, with an opening in its roof. In this chamber were human bones and hair.

As for its being Whittington's own house, it seems improbable. One cannot believe that he lived outside his own parish, so far from his church, where his wife was buried, and for which he did so much. Also the site of his college points to the fact that he lived near Tower Royal and College Hill.

As regards his trade, we know that he supplied the Princess Blanche, eldest daughter of Henry IV., on the occasion of her marriage, with the materials for her wedding dresses, in cloth of gold, at the cost of £215 13s. 4d.; that he also supplied the Princess Philippa, her sister, at her wedding, with " pearls and cloth of gold," at the cost of £248 10s. 6d. His charges for the same kind of thing for John, son of the Earl of Strafford, have also been found. He therefore was the Court mercer, and imported and sold such things as cloth of gold, pearls and other jewels, gold embroideries of all kinds, fine stuffs, silks, and satins set with precious stones and finely worked. Perhaps he sent out in the ships which brought this merchandise home from foreign seas such English exports as wool and home-made cloth, honest and strong. It was a time of great splendour in dress. The extravagance of Richard the Second set an example to the whole Court, and there were no doubt very large profits made in trading with these reckless nobles, who knew nothing of what things cost, nor had any idea of beating down a merchant. It would be curious, could one ever by any inquiry learn, to know how much the Princess Philippa's "cloth of gold" actually did cost Sir Richard Whittington, and what profit he made by the transaction. His investments—for, though there were no banks, the money was not all kept in boxes—were made on the security of laces, jewellery, and other valuable property. Thus he got Lippicote, by making that loan, of which I have already spoken, to his uncle, Philip Mansel. He lent £166 to one of the Scrope family, "Seigneur de Alan;" he lent Henry IV. the sum of £1,000; and when Henry V. came to the City for a second loan, Whittington advanced him £1,000 as his share. All these advances were so many investments. No doubt he also advanced money to assist his fellow-citizens, on security of title-deeds, leases, and stock-in-trade. Before the establishment of banks, all rich men were bankers, advanced money on security, lent on mortgage, received the money of others, and out of money, as well as by buying and selling, made more money.

A gentleman by birth, a rich and successful man, happy in his marriage, a sturdy stickler for justice and liberty, a loyal and patriotic man—so much we have found Whittington. There remains more. We have to show how much he was in advance of his own time in foresight and wisdom for the future.

First, however, of his religion and his friends.

It is asserted by Fox that the opinions of Wycliffe were held, more or less openly, by very many of the foremost London citizens. It is also certain that, in the year 1393, the Archbishop of York and the Bishop of Salisbury complained formally to the King of the Mayor, Aldermen, and Sheriffs of London, Whittington being then Sheriff. They were accused of being "*male creduli*," that is, of little faith towards God and the traditions of their forefathers; they were upholders of Lollards, detractors of religious persons, detainers of tithes, and defrauders of the poor. Considering the charitable disposition of one, at least, among them, one is inclined to believe that the last charge was thrown in merely as a makeweight or elegant rounding off of the sentence, and that the detention of tithes was the thing which most rankled in the minds of the orthodox. Yet, when the burning of heretics began, not a single London citizen of any note was charged with heresy. Perhaps they all hastened, at the least suspicion of danger and the scent of burning wood, to make their submission and peace with the Church. It seems, however, most probable that there was, among the better sort of citizens, a general feeling that the lives of the priests, monks, and religious persons of all kinds were a scandal to religion, and that their ignorance was a cause of great evils to the Church. Among a few, there was a hope that the more glaring superstitions might be removed by more general and more enlightened education. Thus, not only did Whittington promote the cause of learning by the foundation of his library at Grey Friars and Guildhall, but John Carpenter, his executor, formed the City of London School; Sir John Niel, his friend, Master of the Hospital of St. Thomas of Acon, in Chepe, petitioned the Parliament for leave to establish four schools; Sir William Sevenoke founded a grammar school for his native town of Sevenoaks; and Whittington's own company, shortly after his death, founded their school, the Mercers' School, which still exists, and does good work.

If the Bishops suspected those who desired the spread of education, then, without doubt, they suspected Whittington and all his works — his friends, and all their aims. But one need not think so meanly of the Bishops; and, except for this desire and enthusiasm for learning, everything points to the conclusion that Whittington was a firm supporter of orthodoxy. A Lollard, and one who sympathised with Lollardism, would not have bought and presented to the Corporation of London, as Whittington did, the advowson of the oldest city church—that of St. Peter's, Cornhill; nor would a

Lollard and favourer of heresy have rebuilt, at his own charges, the Church of St. Michael, Paternoster Royal. And, as we shall presently see, his will breathes a spirit of profound faith in the ordinances and power of the Church. The truth is, probably, that Whittington had education enough to make him humble as regards his powers of interpreting Scripture. The questioning of doctrine was not in vogue when he was a boy; the teachings of the Church were then accepted without reasoning or doubt, and the new-fangled theories would probably be a subject of disturbance and annoyance to him. Yet he could not but see that the clergy of the country—their immorality, their ignorance, and their luxury—brought contempt upon religion.

As regards his friends and contemporaries, it is interesting to note how many great and remarkable men lived in his time. On the Continent were Dante, Boccaccio, Huss, Froissart; in England were Wycliffe, Chaucer, Gower, Occleve, Lydgate, John de Trevisa, Ralph Higden, William of Wykeham, Walsingham, Fabian, Mandeville, Fortescue, and others. Whether this London merchant knew any of them personally, we cannot say. Froissart came to England at the end of Richard the Second's reign. In his younger days, Whittington may have met with Chaucer in his official capacity of Controller of the Customs; but Chaucer was twenty years older than he, and belonged to the

generation of John of Gaunt. Chaucer also was a
friend of John of Northampton. It is most likely
that Whittington belonged to the Conservative side.
At all events, while John of Northampton's efforts at
reform were being made, Whittington was busily
engaged in looking after the growth of his own
fortune. There is nothing in any of the works of
Chaucer, or those of Gower (also a London poet),
or of Lydgate, to show that Whittington or any of
the Mayors of London was a patron of literature.
But, besides these, there were men of note among the
city worthies of his day whom it is well to mention,
were it only out of respect to their memories.

Among his friends should be certainly reckoned
those great patriots, Sir John Philpot and Sir William
Walworth, though these were both a great deal older
than himself. Of those actually his contemporaries
may be mentioned Sir William Sevenoke, grocer, and
Mayor in 1419—a man who has the honour of being
the first on the long list of London citizens who are
distinguished as founders of grammar schools—he
founded a school in his native place of Sevenoaks, in
Kent; Sir Robert Chichele, grocer, Mayor in 1411
and 1422 (there were three brothers of this name—
one Henry, the Archbishop of Canterbury and
founder of All Souls, Oxford; one William, Sheriff
of London in 1409; and the other this Robert, who
appointed by his will that on his commemoration day

2,400 poor householders of the City should be regaled
at a dinner, and every man to have twopence in
money); Sir John Rainwell, Mayor in 1427, who
gave lands and houses to discharge the tax called the
Fifteenth for three parishes—viz., Billingsgate, Dowgate, and Aldgate ; Sir John Wells, who brought
water from Tyburn ; and Sir William Estfield, who
also made a conduit of water from Highbury to
Cripplegate.   Among those personal friends of Whittington whose names have survived are, first, John
Carpenter, Town Clerk to the City, and the author of
the *Liber Albus*, the most valuable and important
work ever undertaken for any city.   It was commenced at the instigation of Whittington, and completed in his third and last year of office as Mayor.
It is a complete collection of all the laws, customs,
usages, privileges, and rights of the City of London.
The book has been translated by Mr. Riley, and the
life of the author has been written with great care by
Mr. Brewer, formerly Secretary to the City of London
School, which owes its origin to a bequest made by
the same Carpenter, which provided for the maintenance and education of four poor men's children.
Carpenter was one of Whittington's executors, and
appears to have discharged his trust with the greatest
fidelity and conscientiousness.   Sir John Niel, Master
of the Hospital of St. Thomas de Acon, in Chepe, was
another of Whittington's later friends.   He it was

who proposed to establish four grammar schools in
the parishes of All Hallows the Great; St. Andrew,
Holborn; St. Peter, Cornhill; and St. Mary, Cole-
church. Then Alderman John Coventry (Mayor in
1425), an ancestor of the present Earl of Coventry,
was another of Whittington's executors. We may
number among his friends also the learned William
Lichfield, Rector of All Hallows the Great, who
wrote many moral books and 3,083 sermons, all of
which are now, happily, lost. Those who believe
that Whittington was tinged with Lollardism may
strengthen their faith by the fact that Reginald
Pecok was the first master of Whittington's Hospital.
This truly remarkable man was made Bishop of St.
Asaph in 1444, and translated to Chichester in 1449.
His writings upon certain doctrines gave offence, and
he was charged with Lollardism. In the year 1457
he was tried at Lambeth, and convicted of heresy.
By recantation he escaped burning, and after publicly
abjuring his opinions at Paul's Cross, and handing
over fourteen of his books to be burned, he was
sentenced to perpetual imprisonment in Thorney
Abbey, Isle of Ely. He was to be kept in a closed
chamber, out of which he was not allowed to go; no
one was to speak to him, except the man who waited
upon him; he was to have neither paper, pen, nor
ink, nor any books, except a mass-book, a psaltery, a
legendary, and a Bible. A life of Pecok was pub-

lished in 1820 by the Rev. John Lewis. The list of personal friends ends with the name of William Byngham, rector of St. John Zachary. He established a hostel at Cambridge named God's House, in which twenty-four scholars might be trained and educated, to be sent forth to all parts of England, but especially to those places where there were as yet no grammar schools, as missionaries of learning. It was a noble thought, and though God's House was afterwards enlarged and nobly endowed, and became that illustrious and famous college named after Christ, one cannot but lament that a scheme so full of promise should be allowed to die.

It is already clear that Whittington was not alone in his benefactions—in fact, he is but one in a long and illustrious line of London citizens who have considered their wealth a sacred trust, and tried to use it for the good of their fellows. The first of them is Rabere, who built and endowed Bartholomew's; among them are Whittington and Gresham; the last of them is Peabody.

In the fourteenth century two citizens set the example of munificent gifts. The first of them was William Elsinge, a mercer, who founded Elsinge Spital, in the year 1332, for the maintenance of a hundred poor blind men, and afterwards became the first Prior of his own foundation. And in the year 1371, John Barnes gave a chest, secured with three locks, and containing a thousand marks, which were to be lent to young men of the City upon sufficient security. As for those who came after Whittington, their bequests, some of which I have enumerated, were many and great. In 1438 there was a great famine, and the Mayor, Sir Stephen Browne, fitted out at his own expense ships, which brought corn from Prussia, and lowered the price from three shillings a bushel to eighteenpence. Philip Melpas, Sheriff in 1440, gave £125 (equivalent to £1,250 at least of our money) to relieve poor prisoners, with a great quantity of gifts in clothes and money to poor people ; and Robert Large, mercer, to whom Caxton was apprentice, left large sums for improvements in the City, and grants to poor householders. Of later benefactors we need not speak.

Most of Whittington's gifts to the City were made by the provisions of his will. By aid of this document, and by the light of these gifts, we seem enabled to construct a clear idea of the manner of man. It is a procession of dim and cloudy figures which ride along the streets in civic pageant. They have names. Here is the brave Philpot; here the valiant Walworth; here worthy Master Sevenoke; here the great Sir Richard. We know their chains of office, their fur-lined gowns; we see their grave demeanour, but it is hard to catch the features and to know the man. And this we can do, for one at least, by the will which he has left behind him. In this noble document we see how the old man, who has no children, and is alone in the world save for cousins and nephews, feels that he should give back his great fortune to the city where he made it. Great is the power of money; it is like a perennial fountain when it has once been stored up, because it yields its bounty for ever; so that from the thrift of one man may be created, for all after ages, a stream of refreshment and help. "The fervent desire," writes Whittington, when he founded his college, "and busy intention of a prudent, wise, and devout man, should be to cast before and make secure the state and the end of this short life with dedys of mercy and pite, and especially to provide for those miserable persons whom the penurye of poverty insulteth, and to whom the power of seeking the necessaries of life by act or bodily labour is interdicted."

He left nothing of importance to members of his own family, considering, perhaps, that their estates were enough for them; but to his brother he bequeathed a quantity of plate, as if desirous that the memory of his civic distinctions should be kept alive among his kin. Among these things were, "a collour of SS, three dozen of sylver cupps with covers, the one dozen gilt, the second parcel gilt, and the third white; three basins and ewers, three nests of bowls, three flagons, and three livery pots—all of the same material."

The whole of his property was devoted to the great works which he had already commenced or had in his mind. He had already begun the great library which he gave to Grey Friars; he had already laid the foundations of his college; he had rebuilt St. Michael's Church, and had put up his alms-house, called God's House, for thirteen poor men, who were to have each sixteenpence a-week, on the north side of the church. His college was to consist of a Master, four Fellows—who were to be Masters of Arts —clerks and conducts, choristers and servants. The clergy were bound to pray daily for the souls of Sir Richard Whittington and Dame Alice his wife, and for the father and mother of each of them. The licence for the foundation was granted by King Henry IV. in the eleventh year of his reign; and in the twelfth of the same reign, the Mayor and Corporation granted Sir Richard a vacant space of ground whereon to build his college in the Royal.

As for his great Library, the hall which once contained it still stands, and is part of Christ's Hospital. It is 129 feet long and 31 feet broad; it was circled with wainscot, had twenty-eight desks, and eight double settles of wood. In three years after its foundation it was filled with books to the value of £556, of which £400 had been provided by Whittington, and the rest by a friar named Thomas Winchelsey. The great and noble church of the monastery, which contained the bodies of Queen Margaret, Queen Isabella, the Queen of Scots, and an immense number of royal and noble persons, was destroyed by the Great Fire.

Another work of his was the restoration and repairing of the Hospital of St. Bartholomew, which had fallen into decay. A library was also formed here by his bequest.

Again, Guildhall, which was commenced in 1411, and completed in 1421. But it was neither paved nor glazed. This was done by the executors of Whittington. In his own lifetime, as has been stated, he built St. Michael's Church; he also gave largely to the bridge and chapel of Rochester, and to the repair of Gloucester Cathedral. He provided, moreover, drinking fountains, that is to say, he made "bosses" or taps of water in the great aqueduct, a boon of the highest value to the people. And his executors, in accordance with his will, rebuilt and enlarged Newgate Prison, which had grown ruinous, and was foul and fever-stricken.

Lastly, he bequeathed money for a library at the Guildhall, the books of which appear to have been carried away—"borrowed"—by the Duke of Somerset in the reign of Edward VI.

In the same year, his college, which might have been converted into a great place of education, was suppressed. His alms-houses still stand on Highgate Hill, to which place they have been removed.

This record seems to me almost unexampled. There have been many other benefactors to the City, but none so generous, so just, and so far-seeing. Because the people suffered from their want of cleanliness, they should have water. Let them learn to use it. Because poor prisoners suffered from fever in the prison, and sick persons from the want of accommodation in the hospital, let both be rebuilt. Because ignorance is the parent of most evils, let there be libraries, colleges, and schools. Because the more splendid, the more glorious London was, the more jealous of his privileges would be the Londoner, let money be given to beautify Guildhall and build churches. And because the ways of fortune are uncertain, and many a good man is often reduced to poverty by no fault of his own, let there be built almshouses for the reception of those who have failed in the struggle, so that to the sting of defeat may not be added the bitterness of want.

Such were the bequests by which a great merchant in those days sought to mark in a pious fashion his gratitude to God for a long and honourable career, and to make his wealth a blessing for ever to posterity, to keep his memory green — surely a worthy ambition—and to set an example of benevolence as well as of thrift to those who should come after. His college, which should have been converted

into a great High School for the City, is swept away
and destroyed long since ; only the memory of it survives in the name of the street where it stood.   His
church is burned down, and his splendid tomb is
reduced to ashes.   His house, after standing for
four hundred years, is pulled down.   His alms-
houses have been taken away from the City.   The
library which he built for a monastery has fitly
become the hall of London's most famous school ;
there is a noble library at Guildhall, but it is not of
his foundation.   The hospital which Rahere founded,
and Whittington restored, is still full of life and
strength, a place of healing and a school of medicine.
That it is so is due to Whittington ; yet the ungrateful
City has forgotten him, and when they put up statues
to their worthies, they forget the worthiest of all.
The greatest citizen of London is without honour in
his own city.   As well have been a prophet !

It is not given to any man to be very far in
advance of his age.   We see that Whittington was
impressed chiefly with the want of education, the
necessity of providing libraries, the want of water,
the condition of the prisons, and the relief of the poor.
It is also clear, from his official acts and those of his
time, that the City officers were constantly endeavouring to pass good and righteous laws, to administer
justice equally, and to put down disorders.   It was a

day of small things—a time of petty interference and little laws, vexatious, hard to enforce, and based upon ill-understood principles. The close protection of industry, the overlapping of the trades, the never-ending attempts of one man to overreach another, seemed to necessitate enactments which, as they did not perceive, needed a standing force of police to render effective. For instance, no laws could be more useful than those which forbade shooting rubbish into the city ditch ; but who was there to enforce the law ? It was not to be expected that Whittington should perceive what was only discovered four hundred years later—that a town must be guarded and laws enforced by a police which never sleeps ; and, further, that the fewer the laws the better chance of order ; also, it would certainly have been better had Whittington been so far in advance of his age as to have founded a college of sanitary science rather than a college of praying priests.

The four executors of Whittington were John Coventry (already mentioned), who was Sheriff in the year 1417, Mayor in 1425, and died in 1429 ; John Carpenter, Town Clerk (already mentioned) ; James White, clerk ; and William Grove. A curious plate is reproduced by Lysons and by Brewer (" Life of John Carpenter") representing the death of Whittington. He lies, a figure emaciated with age, propped up by pillows. Round him are the four executors,

N

one of them—John Carpenter—holding up his hands in admiration. He is dictating the terms of his will ; his almsmen are gathered together at the foot of the bed, and beside them stands the physician. The picture appears intended to give the portraits of those present. All the faces are distinct and characteristic. John Carpenter, who is known to have been a man of short stature, is represented as hardly reaching to the shoulder of John Coventry, by whom he stands. The face of the dying man is evidently not drawn at hazard, but from recollection of Whittington's thin, strongly-marked features. He was buried in his own Church of St. Michael's, Paternoster Royal, and was covered by a splendid tomb. But tomb and church alike were destroyed in the Great Fire.

The following was his epitaph :—

> " Ut fragrans nardus
> Famâ fuit iste Ricardus
> Albificans Villam,
> Qui juste rexerat illam,
> Flos mercatorum,
> Fundator presbyterorum,
> Sic et egenorum,
> Testis sit certus eorum
> Omnibus exemplum
> Barathrum vincendo morosum
> Condidit hoc templum
> Michaelis quam speciosum,

Regia spes et pres
Divinis res rata turbis;
Pauperibus pater
Et Major qui fuit urbis.
Martius hunc visit
En annos gens tibi dicet,
Finiit ipse dies
Sis sibi Christe quies.   Amen."

His body was three times disturbed, Stow says. First, his executors moved it into a " fair monument ;" next, a certain parson of the church, in the time of Edward VI., sacrilegiously opened the grave, expecting to find treasure, but only found the leaden sheet in which the body was rolled ; this he took away— the greedy creature !   Later on, by order of Queen Mary, the body was lapped in lead as before.

Although the fire swept away church and tomb, the true monument to Whittington is the vast and splendid city, with its navies covering every sea, and its merchants dwelling in every port, which has grown out of his narrow and cramped city, whose people were so free and so presumptuous, and whose merchants were so princely.

His own city is no more ; the narrow streets remain, but the high gables, the frowning halpaces, the carved woodwork, the sculptured stone, the signs built up in the doors, the dark stalls—all these have gone ; warehouses take their places.   His churches, all glorious with precious work, have been burned down; those that have taken their places are empty and deserted. Joy and mirth have left the streets: when the toilers go away, they are silent and deserted. The prentice lads run out no more after every passing show; nor do the damsels dance in the streets at eve for the prize of a flower wreath. Yet the spirit of the City is the same; and wherever an English-speaking town is built, the spirit which Whittington maintained—the love of law, order, and liberty—fills the hearts of the citizens. Wherefore let every English-speaking town respect the name of Whittington, and especially London, "as in private duty bound," and because the glorious City is in a sense, which no other city can boast, the Monument raised to Freedom by her noble citizens.

> " Thy famous Maire, by sure governance,
>   With sword of Justice thee ruleth prudently :
> No lord of Paris, Venice, or Florence,
>   In dignity or honour goeth him nigh.
> He is example, right Lode-star and Guy,
>   Principal patron and Rose originall :
> Above all Maires as master most worthy :
>   LONDON, THOU ART THE FLOWER OF CITIES ALL."

APPENDIX I.

1403. William Askham.		1414. Thomas Fauconer.
1404. John Hende.		1415. Nicolas Wotton.
1405. John Woodcock.		1416. Henry Barton.
1406. Richard Whittington.		1417. Richard Merlawe.
1407. William Staunden.		1418. William Sevenoke.
1408. Drew Barentyn.		1419. Sir Richard Whitting-
1409. Richard Merlawe.		ton.
1410. Thomas Knolles.		1420. William Cambridge.
1411. Robert Chichele.		1421. Sir Robert Chichele.
1412. William Walderne.		1422. Sir Wm. Waldern.
1413. William Cromer.		1423. William Cromer.

APPENDIX II.

The following is a list of some of the noble and great families descended from citizens of London :—

Earl of Coventry—John Coventry, mercer, Mayor in 1425.

Rich—Earl of Warwick and Holland. Richard Rich, mercer, Sheriff, 1441.

Holles—Earls of Clare and Dukes of Newcastle (extinct, 1711)—Sir William Holles, Mayor, 1540.

Lord Leigh—Sir Thomas Leigh, Mayor in 1558.

Earl of Chichester (extinct)—   Do.   do.

Pleydell Bouverie—Edward de Bouverie, Turkey merchant; died 1694.

Lord Ducie—Sir Robert Ducie, Mayor in 1631.

Lord Banning of Sudbury—Paul Banning, Sheriff, 1593.

Cranfield, Earl of Middlesex—Lionel Cranfield.

Ingram, Viscount Irwin—Hugh Irwin, tallow chandler; died 1612.

Sir Stephen Brown, grocer, Mayor, 1438, 1448, father to Sir Antony Brown, Viscount Montague, 1854.

Legge, Lord Dartmouth — First Earl descended from Legge, Lord Mayor, 1347, 1354.

Sir Geoffrey Bullen, Mayor, 1458, grandfather to Thomas, Earl of Wiltshire, who was the father of Anne Bullen.

First Lord Campden—Sir Baptist Hicks, mercer. Built
Hicks's Hall.

Capel, Earl of Essex—Sir William Capel, draper, Mayor,
1503 ; first set up a cage in every ward for the punishment of idle people.

Michael Dormer, Mayor, 1542—from him Lord Dormer.

Edward Osborn, Mayor, 1583—Duke of Leeds.

Earl Craven, descended from Sir William Craven, Mayor,
1611.

Lord Dudley and Ward, descended from William Ward,
jeweller to Henrietta.

APPENDIX III.

The following list is taken from Brewer's "Life of Carpenter." It is curious as showing the literature read by
grave and studious citizens at the time of Whittington.

1. "Alanus de Anticlaudianus."

The "Anticlaudianus" was a Latin poem in nine
books, treating of the seven arts and sciences and on
morals. Alanus de Insulis—Alan de l'Isle—a school-
man, poet, and divine, died in 1202. He was the
author of many works.

2. "Alanus de Planctu Naturæ."

The "Plaint of Nature." By the same author.

3. "De meditationibus et orationibus Sancti Anselmi."

4. A book on architecture, given him by William Cleve.

5. A book "cum secretis Aristotelis," given him by
Marchant.

6. "Liber de regimine dominorum," otherwise called
"Secretum Secretorum Aristotelis."

7. "De Corpore Pollecie."

An English translation was printed in 1521, called
the "Body of Policye."

9. "De Miseria conditionis humanæ."

Written by Cardinal Lotario, afterwards Pope Innocent the Third.

10. " De remediis utriusque fortunæ."

Written in Latin by Petrarch in 1358.

11. " Dispositio et regimen bellorum duorum et acierum Guerrarum."

12. A book " contra duodecim errores et hereses Lollardorum."

Written by the Dominican Roger Dymok in the reign of Richard the Second, and attached to the gate of Westminster Hall on the assemblage of Parliament for all to read.

13. " Ecclesiasticus."

14. " Historiæ Provinciarum."

15. " Law-book of Forms and Precedents."

16. " Philiboblon Ricardi Dunelmensis."

Written in praise of books about the year 1343 by Richard de Bury, Bishop of Durham.

17. " Prosperus de vita contemplativa."

St. Prosperus was a learned scholar of Aquitaine, living A.D. 407–463, and secretary to the Pope, Leo the Great. This work of his is mentioned by Petrarch as being a school-book in his day.

18. " Quidam de Vetula."

A hexameter poem attributed formerly to Ovid.

19. " Seneca ad Callionem."

20. " Seneca de quatuor virtutibus cardinalibus."

21. " Sententiæ divinorum prophetarum." By Peter de Alphonse.

Peter Alphonsus was a converted Jew, who published about the year 1106 a dialogue in defence of Christianity.

22. "De Parabolis Solomonis."
23. "Speculum morale regium."

    A compilation from Thomas Aquinas and other theologians.

24. A book of theology containing the Ten Commandments, the twelve articles of faith, the seven theological virtues, and other things.

There is not among the worthy town clerk's library one single volume of *belles lettres*, unless the "Quidam de Vetula" is one. Not a single book of modern verse, either in French or English ; no romances ; no amusing books of any kind. But the author of "Liber Albus" could not have been a person requiring relaxation of light literature.

APPENDIX IV.

The Legend of Sir Richard Whittington.

———•———

THE HISTORY OF SIR RICHARD WHITTINGTON, THRICE LORD MAYOR OF LONDON.

Printed and Sold in London. (No Date.)

———

THE HISTORY OF SIR RICHARD WHITTINGTON.

CHAP. I.—OF WHITTINGTON'S OBSCURE BIRTH AND HARD FORTUNE, AND OF HIS BEING DROVE TO LONDON.

ONE RICHARD WHITTINGTON, supposed to have been an outcast, for he did not know his parents, they either dying or leaving him to the parish of Taunton Dean, in Somersetshire ; but as he grew up, being displeased with the cruel usage of the nurse, he ran away from her at seven years of age, and travelled about the country, living upon the charity of well-disposed persons, till he grew up to be a fine sturdy youth ; when at last, being threatened to be whipped if he continued in that idle course of life, he resolved to go to London, having heard that the streets were paved with gold. Not knowing the way, he followed the carriers, and at night, for the little service he did them in rubbing the horses, they gave him a supper. When he arrived in this famous city, the carriers, supposing he would be a troublesome hanger-on, told him plainly he must leave the inn and immediately seek out some employment, giving him a groat. With this he wandered about, but, not knowing any one, and being in tattered garb, some pitied him as a forlorn wretch, but few gave him anything.

What he had got being soon spent, his stomach craved supply ; but not having anything to satisfy it, he resolved rather to starve than steal. After two hungry days, and lying on the hulks at night, weary and faint, he got to a merchant's house in Leadenhall Street, where he made many signs of his distressed condition ; but the ill-natured cook was going to kick him from the door, saying, " If you tarry here, I will kick you into the kennel." This put him almost into despair, so he laid him down on the ground, being unable to go any farther. In the meantime, Mr. Fitz-Warren, whose house it was, came from the Royal Exchange, and, seeing him there in that condition, demanded what he wanted, and sharply told him if he did not immediately depart he would cause him to be sent to the House of Correction, calling him a lazy, idle fellow. On this he got up, and, after falling two or three times through faintness for want of food, and making a bow, told him he was a poor country fellow in a starving condition, and if that he might be put in a way, he would refuse no labour, if it was only for his victuals. This raised a Christian compassion in the merchant towards him, and then, wanting a scullion, he immediately ordered one of his servants to take him in, and gave orders how he should be employed ; and so he was feasted to his great refreshment.

[There is no Chap. II. But there is no omission ; it is evidently a mere mistake in numbering.]

Chap. III.—Of Mrs. Alice putting him under the
Cook; of her Cruel Usage to him, and Mrs.
Alice's Interposition in his Favour.

This was the first step of Providence to raise him to what
in time made him to be the City's glory and the nation's
wonder. But he meets with many difficulties, for the
servants make sport of him, and the ill-natured cook told
him, " You are to come under me, so look sharp ; clean the
spit and the dripping-pan, make the fires, wind up the jack,
and nimbly do all other scullery work that I may set you
about, or else I will break your head with my ladle, and
kick you about like a football."

This was cold comfort, but better than starving ; and
what gave him a beam of hope was Mrs. Alice, his master's
daughter, who, hearing her father had entertained a new
servant, came to see him, and ordered that he should
be kindly used. After she had discoursed with him
about his kindred and method of life, and found his
answers ingenuous, she ordered him some cast-off garments,
and that he should be cleaned, and appear like a servant in
the house. Then she went to her parents, and gave them
her opinion of this stranger, which pleased them well,
saying, " He looks like a serviceable fellow to do kitchen
drudgery, run on errands, clean the shoes, and do such
other things as the rest of the servants think beneath them."
By this he was confirmed in his place, and a flock bed pre-
pared in the garret for him. These conditions pleased
him, and he showed great diligence in the work, rising
early and sitting up late, leaving nothing undone that he
could do. But his being mostly under the cook-maid, she
gave him sour sauce to these little sweets ; for she, being of

a morose temper, used her authority beyond reason, so that to keep in the family he had many a broken head, bearing it patiently ; and the more he tried with good words to dissuade her from her cruelty, the more she insulted him, and not only abused him, but frequently complained against him, endeavouring to get him turned out of his service. But Mrs. Alice, hearing of her usage, interposed in his favour, so that she should not prevail against him.

CHAP. IV.—OF HIS BEING TROUBLED WITH VERMIN IN HIS GARRET ; OF HIS BUYING A CAT TO DESTROY THEM ; AND OF HIS SENDING HER FOR A VENTURE ABROAD.

THIS was not the only misery he suffered, for, lying in a place for a long time unfrequented, such abundance of rats and mice had bred there, that they were almost as troublesome by night as the cook was by day, running over his face and disturbing him with their squeaking, so that he knew not what to think of his condition, or how to mend it. After many disquieting thoughts, he at last comforted himself with the hope that the cook might soon marry, or die, or quit her service ; and as for the rats and mice, a cat would be an effectual remedy against them. Soon after, a merchant came to dinner, and it raining exceedingly, he staid all night, whose shoes Whittington having cleaned, and presented at his chamber door, he gave him a penny. This stock he improved, for, going along the street of an errand, he saw a woman with a cat under her arm ; so he desired to know the price of it ? The woman praised it for a good mouser, and told him sixpence ; but he declaring that a penny

was all his stock, she let him have it. This he brought
home, and kept in a box all day, lest the cook should kill
her if she came into the kitchen ; and at night he set
her to work for her living. Puss delivered him from one
plague, but the other remained, though not for many
years.

It was the custom with the worthy merchant, Mr. Hugh
Fitz-Warren, that God might give him a greater blessing to
his endeavours, to call all his servants together when he
sent out a ship, and cause every one to venture something
in it, to try their fortunes, for which they were to pay
nothing for freight or custom.

Now all but Whittington appeared, and brought things
according to their abilities ; but Mrs. Alice being by, and
supposing that poverty made him decline coming, she
ordered him to be called, on which he made several excuses.
However, being constrained to come, he fell upon his knees,
desiring them not to jeer a poor simple fellow, in expectation that he was going to turn merchant, since all that he
could lay claim to as his own was but a poor cat, which
he had bought for one penny he had given him for cleaning
shoes, which had much befriended him in keeping the rats
and mice from him. Upon this Mrs. Alice proffered to lay
something down for him ; but her father told her the
custom, it must be his own which he ventured, and
ordered him to fetch his cat, which he did, but with great
reluctance, fancying nothing could come of it, and with
some tears delivered her to the master of the ship, which
was called the *Unicorn,* and was to sail down to Blackwall,
in order to proceed on her voyage.

CHAP. V.—OF WHITTINGTON'S ELOPEMENT ON ALL HAL-
LOWS' DAY, AND HIS RETURN ON HEARING BOW
BELLS RING ; AND OF THE DISPOSAL OF THE CAT BY
THE FACTOR ABROAD.

THE cook-maid, who little thought how advantageous
Whittington's cat would prove, when she did not scold at
him, would jeer him about his grand adventure, and led
him such a life that he grew weary of enduring it, and, little
expecting what ensued, resolved rather to try Dame Fortune
than live in such great torment ; and so, having packed up
his bundle over night, got out early on All Hallows' Day,
intending to ramble the country. But as he went through
Moorfields, he began to have pensive thoughts, and his
resolutions began to fail. However, on he went to Hol-
loway, and sat down to consider the matter, when, on a
sudden, Bow Bells began to ring a merry peal. He, listen-
ing, fancied they called him back from his intended journey,
and promised him the good fortune which afterwards befel
him, imagining they expressed—

> Turn again, Whittington,
> Lord Mayor of London.

This was a happy thought for him, as it made so great an
impression on him that, finding it early, and that he might
be back before the family were stirring, he delayed not ; and
all things answered his expectation, for, having left the door
ajar, he crept softly in, and got to his usual drudgery.

During this time, the ship in which the cat was, by contrary winds, was driven on the coast of Barbary, inhabited
by the Moors, unknown to the English ; but finding the
people courteous, the Master and Factor traded with them ;

O

so, bringing their wares of sundry sorts upon deck and opening them, they pleased them so well that the news was carried to the King, who sent for patterns, with which he was so pleased that he sent for the Factor to his palace. Their entertainment, according to custom, was on the floor, covered with carpets interwoven with gold and silver, cross-legged. This kind of table was no sooner covered with various dishes but the scent drew together a great number of rats and mice, who devoured all that came in the way; which surprised the Factor, who asked the nobles if these vermin were not offensive? "O," said they, "His Majesty would give half his revenue to be freed from them, for they are not only offensive at his table, but his chamber and bed are so troubled with them, that he is always watched for fear of mischief." The Factor, then, remembering Whittington's cat, and rejoicing at the occasion, told them that he had an English beast in the ship that would rid all the Court of them quickly. The King, overjoyed at the good news, and being anxious to be freed from those vermin which so much spoiled his pleasure, disturbed his mind, and made all his enjoyments dissatisfactory and burdensome, desired to see this surprising creature, saying, "For such a thing I will load your ship with gold, diamonds, and pearls." This large offer made the Master endeavour the more to enhance the cat's merits, saying, "She is the most admirable creature in the world, and I cannot spare her, for she keeps my ship clear of them, otherwise they would destroy all my goods." But His Majesty would take no denial, saying, "No price shall part us." The cat being sent for, and the tables spread, the vermin came as before. Then, setting her on the table, she fell to immediately, and killed them all in a trice; then she came purring and curling up her tail to the King and Queen, as if she asked a reward for her service; whilst they admired her, protesting it was the finest diversion they had ever seen.

CHAP. VI.—OF THE RICHES RECEIVED FOR THE CAT; THE UNBELIEF OF WHITTINGTON ON THEIR ARRIVAL; AND OF HIS LIBERALITY TO SOME OF HIS FELLOW-SERVANTS.

THE Moorish King was so pleased with the cat, especially when the Master told him she was with young, and would stock the whole country, that he gave ten times more for the cat than all the freight besides. So they sailed with a fair wind, and arrived safe at Blackwall, being the richest ship that ever came into England. The Master taking the cabinet of jewels with him, they being too rich a prize to be left on board, presented his bill of lading to Fitz-Warren, who praised God for such a prosperous voyage. But when he called all his servants to give each his due, the Master showed him the cabinet of jewels and pearls, the sight of which much surprised him; but on being told it was all for Whittington's cat, he said, "God forbid that I should deprive him of one farthing of it;" and so he sent for him by the title of Mr. Whittington, who was then in the kitchen cleaning of pots and spits. Being told he must come to his master, he made several excuses; but being urged to go, he at length came to the door, and there stood scringing and scraping, scrupling to enter, till the merchant commanded him in, and ordered a chair to be immediately set for him; on which he, thinking they intended to make sport with him, fell on his knees, and with tears in his eyes besought them not to mock a simple fellow who meant none of them any harm. Mr. Fitz-Warren, raising him up, said, "Indeed, Mr. Whittington, we are serious with you, for in estate at this instant you are an abler man than myself;" and then gave him the vast riches, which amounted to three hundred thousand pounds, an immense sum in those days.

At length, being persuaded to believe, he fell upon his knees and praised Almighty God, who had vouchsafed to behold so poor a creature in the midst of his misery. Then, turning to his master, he laid his riches at his feet; but he said, "No, Mr. Whittington; God forbid I should take so much as a ducat from you; may it be a comfort to you." Then he turned to Mrs. Alice, but she also refused it; upon which, bowing low, he said unto her, "Madam, whenever you please to make choice of a husband, I will make you the greatest fortune in the world."

Upon this he began to distribute his bounty to his fellow-servants, giving even his mortal enemy the cook one hundred pounds for her portion; she saying she was in her passion, he freely forgave her. He also distributed his bounty very plentifully to all the ship's crew.

CHAP. VII.—OF MR. WHITTINGTON'S COMELY PERSON AND DEPORTMENT; OF MRS. ALICE'S FALLING IN LOVE WITH HIM AND MARRYING HIM; AND OF HIS BEING SHERIFF OF LONDON.

UPON this change, the haberdashers, tailors, and sempstresses were set to work to make Mr. Whittington's cloaths, all things answerable to his fortune. Being dressed, he appeared a very comely person, insomuch that Mrs. Alice began to lay her eyes upon him. Now her father, seeing this, intended a match for them, looking upon him to be a fortunate man. He also took him to the Royal Exchange, to see the customs of the merchants, where he was no sooner known than they came to welcome him into their society. Soon after, a match was proposed between him and his master's daughter, when he excused himself on account of the meanness of his birth; but that objection being removed by his present worth, it was soon agreed on, and the Lord Mayor and Aldermen invited to the wedding.

After the honeymoon was over, his father-in-law asked him what employment he would follow? Whereupon he replied he should think of that of a merchant. So they joined together in partnership, and both grew immensely rich.

Though fortune had thus bountifully smiled on the subject of our history, he was far from proud, yet merry, which made his company and acquaintance courted by all; and in a short time he was nominated Sheriff of London, in the year 1040, Sir John Haddle then being Lord Mayor.

CHAP. VIII.—OF HIS BEING THRICE LORD MAYOR; HIS ENTERTAINMENT OF HENRY V.; AND HIS DEATH AND BURIAL.

THUS he grew in riches and fame, greatly beloved by all, especially the poor, whose hunger he always supplied.

In four years he was chosen Lord Mayor, in which office he behaved with such justice and prudence that he was chosen in the same office twice afterwards. In the same year he entertained King Henry V., after his conquest of France, and his Queen, in such a very grand manner, that he was pleased to say that never king had such a subject, and conferred upon him the honour of knighthood. At this entertainment the King particularly praised the fire,

which was made of choice wood, mixed with mace, cinna-
mon, and all other spices; on which Sir Richard said he
would endeavour to make one still more agreeable to His
Majesty, and immediately tore and threw into the fire the
King's bond for 10,000 marks, due to the Company of
Mercers; 2,500 to the Chamber of London; 2,000 to the
Grocers; to the Merchants, Staplers, Goldsmiths, Haberdashers, Vintners, Brewers, and Bakers, 3,000 each. "All
these," said Sir Richard, "with divers others, lent for the
payment of your soldiers in France, I have taken in and
discharged, to the amount of £60,000 sterling. Can your
Majesty desire to see such another sight?" The King and
nobles were struck dumb at his wealth and liberality.

Sir Richard spent the rest of his days honoured by the
rich and beloved by the poor. He had by his wife two
sons and two daughters, some of whose posterity are worthy
citizens. He built many charitable houses; also a church
in Vintry Ward dedicated to St. Michael, adding to it a
college founded to St. Mary, with a yearly allowance for the
poor scholars; near which he erected an hospital, called
God's House, and well endowed it. There he caused his
father and mother-in-law to be buried, and left room for
himself and his wife when death should call them. He
built Newgate, a place for criminals. He gave large sums
to Bartholomew's Hospital, and to many other charitable
uses.

Dame Alice, his wife, died in the 63rd year of her age,
after which he would not marry, though he outlived her near
twenty years. In the conclusion, he was buried in the
place aforesaid, leaving a good name to posterity; and the
following epitaph was written on his tomb, and continued
perfect till destroyed by the Fire of London :—

Their Epitaph.

Here lies Sir Richard Whittington, thrice Mayor,
And his dear wife, a virtuous loving pair ;
Him fortune raised to be beloved and great,
By the adventure only of a cat.
Let none that read it of God's love despair,
Who trusts in Him, He will of him take care ;
But growing rich, chuse humbleness, not pride ;
Let these dead virtuous persons be your guide.

A SONG.

Sir Richard Whittington.

Here I must tell the praise of worthy Whittington,
Known to be in his days Lord Mayor of London.
But of poor parents born was he, we hear,
And in his youth brought up in Somersetshire.
Poorly, then, up to London came this simple lad,
And with a merchant soon a dwelling had ;
And in the kitchen plac'd, a scullion for to be,
And a long time he passed in labour drudgingly.
His daily hour was turning spits at the fire,
To scour lats for a poor scullion's hire.
Meat and drink his pay, of coin he had no store
And to run away in secret thus he bore ;
So from the merchant Whittington secretly
Into the country run to purchase liberty,
But as he went along in a fine summer's morn,
London bells sweetly rung, Turn again, Whittington,
Evermore sounding so, Turn again, Whittington,
For thou in time shalt be Lord Mayor of London.

Whereupon back came Whittington with speed,
A servant to remain, as the Lord had decreed.
And blessed be the bells, this was his daily song,
That my good fortune tell; most sweetly have they rung.
If God so favour me, I will not be so unkind,
London my love shall see, and my bounty find.
But for this happy chance, this scullion had a cat,
That did his fame advance, and him wealth gat.
Whittington had no more than his poor cat then,
Which to the ship he bore like a valiant man.
Venturing the same, says he, I may get store of gold,
And the Mayor of London be, the bells have told.
Whittington's merchandise carried upon the land,
Troubled with rats and mice, as we do understand;
The King who there reign'd, as he at dinner sat,
Daily in fear remain'd of many a mouse and rat;
Meat that on trenchers lay, no way could they keep safe,
But by rats torn away, fearing no whip or staff.
Hereupon they brought heaps of gold given for that,
Home again they hie, with their ship laden so,
Whittington's wealth by his cat began to grow.
A scullion's life he forsook to be a merchant good,
And soon began to look how his credit stood.
After he was chose Sheriff of the City we hear,
And then quickly rose, as it doth appear,
For the City's grace, Sir Richard Whittington,
Came to be in his days thrice Lord Mayor of London.
His fame to advance, thousands he lent the King,
To maintain war in France, glory from thence to bring,
And after a feast which he the King did make,
He burnt the note in jest, and would no money take.

Prisoners cherished were, widows comfort found,
Good deeds far and near by him were done ;
Whittington's College is one of his charities,
Newgate he built where many prisoner lies.
Many more deeds were done by Whittington,
Which joy and comfort bring to those who look on.
Somerset, thou hast bred the flower of charity.
Altho' he's dead and gone, yet he lives lastingly.
Call him back no more to live in London,
Those bells that called him back, Turn again, Whittington !

INDEX.

Printed in the United Kingdom by
Lightning Source UK Ltd., Milton Keynes
137347UK00002B/25/A